D1233357

ALAMO

CONSTANTINOPLE

DIEN BIEN PHU

MASADA

PETERSBURG

STALINGRAD

Western Russia

- ⊙ Republic capital
- • City/town
- — International border
- ⸺ Railroad

0 ___ 400 km
0 ___ 300 mi

Norway
Barents Sea
Novaya Zemlya
Kara Sea
Amderma
Novyy Port
Pechenga
Murmansk
Vorkuta
Labytnangi
Nadym
Nar'yan-Mar
White Sea
Mezen'
Pechora
Belomorsk
Arkhangel'sk
Ukhta
Sergino
Finland
Lake Ladoga
Lake Onega
Severnaya Dvina
Vychegda
Ob'
Sweden
Helsinki
Vyborg
Kotlas
Syktyvkar
Krasnovishersk
Severoural'sk
Stockholm
Konosha
Serov
Tallinn
St. Petersburg (Leningrad)
Sukhona
Berezniki
Baltic Sea
Estonia
Vologda
Kirov
Perm'
Nizhniy Tagil
Pskov
Novgorod
Yekaterinburg (Sverdlovsk)
Riga
Latvia
Tver' (Kalinin)
Yaroslavl'
Nizhniy Novgorod (Gor'kiy)
Izhevsk
Chelyabinsk
Kaliningrad
Lithuania
Volga
Moskva
Kazan'
Naberezhnyy Chelny
Ufa
Troitsk
Vilnius
Moscow
Vladimir
Kama
Kartaly
Poland
Minsk
Smolensk
Ryazan'
Simbirsk
Magnitogorsk
Warsaw
Belarus
Tula
Saransk
Tol'yatti
Brest
Gomel'
Bryansk
Penza
Kuznetsk
Samara (Kuybyshev)
Orenburg
Orsk
Vistula
Kovel'
Oka
Orël
Tambov
Don
Ural
Slovakia
Rovno
L'vov
Kiev
Kursk
Voronezh
Saratov
Ural'sk
Aktyubinsk
Hungary
Vinnitsa
Khar'kov
Volga
Kazakhstan
Ukraine
Kremenchug
Dnepropetrovsk
Lugansk
Volgograd
Makat
Moldova
Krivoy Rog
Zaporozh'ye
Donetsk
Volga-Don Canal
Gur'yev
Chisinau
Nikolayev
Taganrog
Rostov
Don
Beyneu
Romania
Odessa
Mariupol (Zhdanov)
Kherson
Astrakhan'
Bucharest
Kerch
Krasnodar
Armavir
Fort Shevchenko
Uzbekistan
Danube
Simferopol'
Constanta
Sevastopol'
Novorossiysk
Shevchenko
Sofia
Groznyy
Caspian Sea
Bulgaria
Black Sea
Georgia
Turkmenistan
Greece
Istanbul
Batumi
Tbilisi
Baku
Krasnovodsk
Ankara
Armenia
Azerbaijan
Yerevan
Athens
Turkey
Iran

©1994 MAGELLAN Geographix℠Santa Barbara CA 1-800-929-4MAP

STALINGRAD

TIM McNEESE

CHELSEA HOUSE
PUBLISHERS
A Haights Cross Communications Company

Philadelphia

FRONTIS Map of Western Russia. Stalingrad (now Volgograd) has
many sites reminding visitors of the pain of World War II.

COVER Red Army troops storming an apartment block amidst the ruins
of Stalingrad during World War II.

CHELSEA HOUSE PUBLISHERS

VP, NEW PRODUCT DEVELOPMENT Sally Cheney
DIRECTOR OF PRODUCTION Kim Shinners
CREATIVE MANAGER Takeshi Takahashi
MANUFACTURING MANAGER Diann Grasse

STAFF FOR STALINGRAD

EXECUTIVE EDITOR Lee Marcott
PRODUCTION EDITOR Jaimie Winkler
PICTURE RESEARCHER Patricia Burns
SERIES & COVER DESIGNER Keith Trego
LAYOUT 21st Century Publishing and Communications, Inc.

A Haights Cross Communications ↗ Company

http://www.chelseahouse.com

First Printing

1 3 5 7 9 8 6 4 2

Library of Congress Cataloging-in-Publication Data

McNeese, Tim.
    Stalingrad / Timothy MCNeese.
        p. cm.—(Sieges that changed the world)
Includes index.
    ISBN 0-7910-7230-4 HC   0-7910-7528-1 PB
  1. Stalingrad, Battle of, Volgograd, Russia, 1942–1943—Juvenile literature.
2. World War, 1939–1945—Campaigns—Soviet Union—Juvenile literature.
I. Title. II. Series.
D764.3.S7 M385 2002
940.54'2147—dc21

                                                                2002012917

TABLE OF CONTENTS

Vladimir Ilyich Lenin, seen here speaking to a crowd at a 1921 celebration, was the revolutionary who led Communist forces after the Russian emperor was removed from his throne. Lenin's efforts helped establish the new Soviet Union.

A Stage Set for War

Fires dotted the bombed-out urban landscape of the Russian city of Stalingrad, on the banks of the Volga River. German troops were attempting to occupy the city, and thousands of Russian street fighters were intent on stopping them. One unit— 1st company, 1st battalion, 42nd regiment, 13th guards—had just been assigned a difficult task by the leader of the Russian 62nd army, General Vassili Chuikov: "Hold the main railroad station."

The 1st company's commander, Lieutenant Anton Kuzmich Dragan assembled his men and headed toward the railroad terminal in the city's Red Square. As they approached, the Germans who had already occupied the station fired at the Russians. Dragan and his men attacked the building. Then, as "grenades exploded, machine-gun tracers split the darkness and suddenly the Germans were gone." The 1st company spread out, taking positions in empty boxcars and cabooses, and waited for the enemy—and the sun—to rise.

Soon, the railroad station was surrounded by Germans on three sides. German planes struck the Russian-occupied station, blowing out the walls and causing the building's iron girders to give way. Too dangerous to remain in the station, Dragan ordered his men to evacuate to a nearby nail factory. Once inside, the Russian lieutenant took inventory and found that he had little food or ammunition. Without enough water to drink, his men fired their machine guns, ripping holes in drainpipes, desperate for anything to ease their thirst. To their dismay, the pipes were empty.

Days passed as Dragan and his beleaguered forces faced a pounding by German tanks and *Luftwaffe* (German air force) planes. The Russian unit moved repeatedly from one half-demolished building to another, as Dragan ordered his men to stand and fight. The battered Russians had little time to note the city landmarks they passed—the bombed-out remnants of a theater, the City Soviet building, the *Pravda* newspaper office, a fountain and statue of children dancing —as they fought their way along the streets of Stalingrad. Under a constant barrage of heavy fire, Dragan led his men to shelter in an apartment basement. Certain that they were surrounded, the Russian officer placed his remaining 40 men at the windows. Again, they waited.

After ten days of fighting, on the morning of September 25, 1942, 1st company had only ten men left. Some members of the company had abandoned their comrades and returned to their headquarters, where they reported that Dragan and his men were all dead. In fact, Dragan was still alive and taking heavy fire from advancing German units. When his men had tossed their last grenades, they began to throw bricks at the approaching enemy. Finally, when they were entirely out of ammunition, the lieutenant and his men prepared to die. One of them scratched some final words on a wall: "Rodimtsev's guardsmen fought and died for their country here." Just then, German tanks, called Panzers, fired point-blank into Dragan's temporary fortress. The building collapsed around the Russians, but, miraculously, seven of the men in the rubble survived. After nightfall, they crawled out, wounded, filthy after days of fighting, and exhausted—but they were still alive.

Through the night, the Russians moved in the shadows toward the Volga River. They dodged several German patrols. More than once, Dragan sent one of his men to stab an unsuspecting German sentry. Each of Dragan's soldiers did his deadly work quietly and efficiently. Finally, the handful of men reached the Volga, where they dropped to its banks and drank heavily. When German patrols discovered them, Dragan and his men fitted logs together and floated out on a makeshift raft into the broad river's current. The following morning, Dragan and his six remaining men reached a Russian artillery unit and safety.

From August 1942, until early February 1943, hundreds of thousands of men—including Russians, Germans, Italians, Romanians, and a host of other ethnic groups—fought a lengthy battle for control of the city on the Volga—Stalingrad. German units surrounded the city from the west and drove relentlessly toward the banks of the river. The number of casualties from the fight would be appalling, and the carnage of the siege laid down by the Germans and the counterattack and encirclement the Russians later made would defy reason.

What drove the Germans, led by a totalitarian dictator named Adolf Hitler, to march 1,500 miles (2,414 kilometers) from their homeland and lay siege to a Russian city that, in the end, had little strategic importance? What mysteries of war can explain why these two immense and seemingly immovable German and Russian forces met in the summer of 1942 and engaged in months of bloody struggle, until one achieved costly victory and the other the humility of total defeat? The siege and battle of Stalingrad is a story of terror and triumph, chaos and courage, viciousness and victory. To modern-day Russians, World War II is remembered as "The Great Patriotic War." The experience of Stalingrad makes no other name more fitting.

To some modern historians, World War I and World War II actually represent the beginning and end of the same conflict. Although the leaders of all of the major combatant nations changed, along with the governments of some of those countries, the end of World War I set Europe on course for a later conflict.

World War I (1914–1918) was an extremely bloody, exhausting struggle. It began because of confusion and rapid escalation after the assassination of the heir to the throne of the Austrian-Hungarian Empire. Through the summer of 1914, the battle lines were drawn, as allies, both large and small, lined up to face one another in a great conflict. Great Britain, France, and Russia formed a three-way alliance to face the ever-increasing bullying and offensive measures taken by the empires of Germany and Austria-Hungary. (By 1915, Italy had joined with the Western powers, while Bulgaria and the Ottoman Empire had sided with Germany and its allies.)

Once hostilities broke out, the war quickly became one of attrition as the two sides fought trench warfare that resulted in the deaths of millions of men on both sides. Many of the battlefields stretched across the remote farm fields of eastern France and Belgium. The warfare was modern in every way for that time. It included new weapons that inflicted utter destruction, including long-range artillery, bomb-dropping airplanes and airships, poison gas, and the weapon that claimed more lives than any other during the four-year-long conflict—the machine gun.

The war, which cost more than any other international conflict before that time, devastated the economies of most of the nations involved. Perhaps chief among them was the empire of the Russian czar, Nicholas II. When fighting broke out, Russia was in no position to fight a war of such massive scale. The conflict went badly for the Russians almost from the beginning. In his book *Russia, A History*, historian Gregory Freeze described the predicament the czar faced by early 1915, after just six months of war:

> German divisions had dealt a string of shattering defeats. Russia's stock of ammunition and weapons was perilously low, neither domestic production nor imports could satisfy the gargantuan demand of this first modern war. . . . By early 1915 one high official declared that Russia could only pray to her patron saints and rely upon her vast spaces and the spring mud to slow the relentless German advance. . . . War, however, proved particularly difficult for Russia, one reason being that the "crisis was at the top"—a mutual alienation that divided state and "Society."

In short, the people of Russia no longer trusted in the leadership of their czar. A revolutionary spirit had begun to develop even before the war, and it did not die during the difficult conflict. Although some people felt it was unpatriotic for Russian revolutionaries to speak of bringing down the Russian government as it struggled to fight the war, by 1917, political extremists did just that. With Russian morale at its lowest and the nation facing a crisis at every turn, a revolution successfully removed Nicholas II from his throne in 1917, and ended royal rule entirely. Before the year's end, Communist revolutionaries had taken control of the Russian government.

The new Communist leadership still had to face the

realities of warfare, however. By the summer of 1918, German armies had occupied a great deal of Russian territory. The troops of the German leader, Kaiser Wilhelm II, had invaded Russian lands as far as the Baltic Sea and were pounding on the gates of the city of Petrograd (formerly called St. Petersburg and later renamed Leningrad). The enemy had surrounded the Russian city of Kiev, capital of the Ukraine, and stood on the shores of the Black Sea at Rostov-on-Don. Along with this territory, German forces controlled "one-third of Russia's population, one-third of its agricultural land and more than one-half of its industry." These territories had not fallen into German hands simply by military advance. The new Communist government, led by a revolutionary named V. I. Lenin, had allowed the annexation of these and other Russian territories under the Treaty of Brest-Litovsk. The agreement had been signed in March 1918 to allow the war-weary Russians to back out of the deadly and destructive conflict it had waged for nearly three years.

Yet, despite German success against the Russians in the East, by August, the Allies were pushing the Germans hard and forced them to surrender significant ground in the West. Overextended and exhausted by war, the German people were experiencing food shortages, largely because of successful Allied blockades at sea. By October, the Germans and the Austrians began to ask for terms to end the war. On November 11, 1918, the leaders of both sides signed an armistice that called for the immediate end to all hostilities.

Even as Lenin took Russia out of World War I, he and his fellow Bolsheviks (Communists) soon faced another fight—this time with their Russian political opponents, those who opposed communism. This civil war lasted from 1918 to 1921. Ultimately, the Bolshevik (or Red) forces of Lenin defeated the White (or anti-Bolshevik) army. By 1921, communism was well entrenched in

Russia, as well as the neighboring regions of the Ukraine, White Russia, the Trans-Caucasia, as well as the distant lands of Siberia. The following year, Lenin's government renamed the nation—the Union of Soviet Socialist Republics (Soviet Union, or USSR).

While Russia plunged into a swirling stream of internal political change, the victors and the defeated powers of World War I prepared to negotiate an official peace treaty in the spring of 1919. By that time, the leaders and people of each country had stepped back to take a hard look at how the war had reduced much of Europe to ruins. Millions of lives had been lost, including 10 million combatants. Two nations had lost the greatest number of people: Germany, with 1.8 million killed, and Russia, with 1.7 million dead. France and Austria-Hungary each lost between 1.2 and 1.3 million, while Great Britain could count nearly one million dead. Approximately 500,000 Italian soldiers had died as well. As the leaders of the Allied nations—Great Britain, France, and Italy—met together at the peace conference held at Versailles, the seventeenth-century palace of French King Louis XIV, they intended to make Germany pay for its role in the war.

During the 1920s, Germany struggled under the limitations of the Versailles Treaty. Its currency became almost worthless, and postwar Germany was plagued with inflation and a mountain of international debt. The new German government, the Weimar Republic, was always unpopular with its people, for it never seemed able to cope with the problems of a poor economy, a lack of political stability, and a weak military. Political extremists constantly rallied and campaigned against the German republican government. These revolutionaries spoke out against the Versailles Treaty and the impossible reparation payments it had forced upon the German government.

Among those who hoped to bring down the weak

government and reestablish a powerful Germany was a veteran of World War I, a Bavarian named Adolf Hitler. As a corporal during the war, Hitler was decorated twice for bravery, had been wounded, and temporarily lost his sight in a poison gas attack near the war's end. In fact, when Germany surrendered in the fall of 1918, Hitler was recovering from his injuries in a hospital. Germany's defeat and the humiliating peace treaty outraged Hitler. Although he took a postwar job with the Weimar Republic government, training military recruits to be loyal to democratic Germany, he did not intend to remain loyal to it himself. As soon as Germany signed the Versailles

A Humiliating Treaty

Under the post–World War I agreement called the Treaty of Versailles, the Allies forced a bitter peace on Germany. The victorious nations placed responsibility for the war firmly on Germany's shoulders, and Germany was punished severely. The treaty took away German territory and redrew the boundaries of the defeated nation. (The territory it had gained from Russia under the Treaty of Brest-Litovsk was returned to the new Russian government.) Germany was also saddled with war damages that amounted to a staggering 132 billion in gold marks (German currency). In addition, the Germans were required to pay some of their debts to the Allied nations in the form of coal shipments.

Having been defeated in war and blamed for the conflict's outbreak, Germany was ordered to dismantle its military, to prevent the nation from starting a future war. The army of the German Empire, which had once numbered in the millions, was reduced to 100,000 men in uniform. The German navy was reduced to six primary warships, and the German submarines—the U-boats that had terrorized ships on the high seas—were destroyed. Germany was allowed to have no warplanes.

The harsh Versailles Treaty was immediately unpopular with the German people. The oppressive reparations and humiliating conditions of the treaty caused much suffering in Germany over the next decade. The people's discontent would help set the stage for yet another war.

Treaty, Hitler recalled in 1936, then "I thought of nothing else than a coup d'etat."

By the early 1920s, Adolf Hitler formed a party of supporters called the National Socialist German Workers Party, known to many as the Nazis. A fiery leader, Hitler spoke out about the enemies of Germany, including the Western powers that had created the Versailles Treaty. He called them the "betrayers of the German Fatherland." He talked bitterly of others, including the Poles, the Slavs of the newly formed nations of Yugoslavia and Czechoslovakia, and of Russian Bolsheviks who supported communism, a system Hitler hated.

When Hitler's Nazi party tried to take over the government of Bavaria, in Austria, the effort failed. Hitler was arrested and sentenced to five years in prison for treason. After he had served less than a year of his sentence, Hitler was released. By this point, he was already on his way to popularity among the German people.

The following year, the Weimar government began to crack down on subversive political groups such as the Nazis. For a while, the party was banned in Germany. When Hitler vowed that he would never again lead a revolt against the government, however, German officials allowed the Nazis to organize publicly once again. Throughout the 1920s, the Nazis gained supporters, as Hitler courted power sources throughout Germany, including the business community, labor unions, captains of industry, and farming interests. By 1929, the Nazi party was the most important and well-known minority political group in Germany. When a serious economic downturn hit Europe in 1930, Hitler was ready to blame specific people— especially Jewish bankers, American capitalists, and Russian Communists. As more and more people in Germany became aware of his message of blame and hate, Hitler became a symbol of their frustration.

During these years, in the Soviet Union, a Communist party official named Joseph Stalin was busy consolidating power for himself. Stalin was known as a man of caution, cunning, and calculation, one who was cruel and would murder his opponents to further his own political position. Just as Adolf Hitler did in Germany, Stalin ordered the death of anyone he believed was standing in his way.

As the 1930s began, the world was experiencing a severe economic depression. At the same time, both Stalin and Hitler had nearly eliminated all their rivals. Stalin's secret police killed hundreds of thousands of his opponents, including members of the Communist party whose loyalty Stalin doubted. By 1932, Hitler and his Nazis were riding a wave of popularity among desperate Germans, and won the majority of seats in the German legislature. Hitler was invited to form a government cabinet controlled by the Nazis. Six months later, in January 1933, the elderly president of the Weimar Republic, Paul von Hindenburg, appointed Hitler as his chancellor, a position similar to a prime minister. Hitler had become the second most power-ful man in the German government.

Systematically, Hitler began to take full control of Germany for himself. Hindenburg, verging on senility, could do little to oppose the popular Nazi leader. Over the next six years, Hitler led the German people exactly where he wanted them to go. Before the end of 1933, he had with-drawn Germany from the international peace organization of the era, the League of Nations. Two years later, he called for Germany to re-arm, while he publicly condemned the Versailles Treaty. In a few short years, he restored the draft and built an army of 500,000 men, many of them loyal to the Nazi party. The following year, he sent his army into the Rhineland, a rich, fertile territory bordering France that had once belonged to Germany. Hitler's invasion of the Rhineland was a direct, calculated military move, one that

German dictator Adolf Hitler (left) formed a partnership with Italian dictator Benito Mussolini (right) in the years leading up to World War II. The two hoped to take control of Europe and run it as they wished.

violated the Versailles Treaty. Even so, as Hitler's newly resurrected German military went on the march, the other powers of Europe—including Great Britain and France—simply stood by and watched.

Before the end of 1936, Hitler formed an alliance with Benito Mussolini, the militaristic dictator of Italy. Their partnership, which they labeled the "Rome-Berlin Axis," was intended to create a Europe that revolved around them. Although Hitler did not like Mussolini personally, and the Italian dictator criticized Hitler when he sent troops into the Rhineland, the two made a cynical agreement to cooperate with one another in further moves of aggression.

Two years later, in 1938, Hitler took command of all German military forces (something he promised he would never do) and ordered them to march against their neighbors to the east. His first target was Germany's neighbor, Austria. The move to take over Austria did not even require a single German soldier. Because there was a strong Nazi organization in Austria (the Nazis there had murdered the Austrian chancellor in 1934), Hitler had only to summon the Austrian premier, Kurt von Schuschnigg to a meeting. There, Hitler bullied Schuschnigg into putting Austrian Nazis in his cabinet. The intimidated Schuschnigg then resigned his post, allowing Hitler to send troops into Austria virtually unopposed. On March 13, 1938, Hitler annexed Austria, making it a German territory. Despite Germany's blatant aggression against one of its neighbors, the democracies of Western Europe—Great Britain and France—once again did nothing, managing only a weak protest.

The Austrian annexation placed Germany in a geographical position to attack Eastern European nations, including Hungary, Yugoslavia, and Czechoslovakia. Hitler began to eye his next target almost immediately—the horseshoe-shaped region of western Czechoslovakia, called the Sudetenland. After it annexed Austria, Germany encircled more than half of Czechoslovakia. Hitler claimed that the region should be part of Germany, since 3 million German-speaking people lived there. Seeing Hitler's aggressive intentions, the Western powers negotiated with him and offered him control of the Sudetenland, in exchange for his promise to make no further invasions. The negotiations—called the Munich Agreement—did not involve any representatives from Czechoslovakia.

Even the annexation of the Sudetenland, with its coal mines, industrial base, iron deposits, and millions of people did not satisfy Hitler's appetite for expansion, however. By March 1939, his army had marched into the rest of Czechoslovakia. Only then did Western European leaders realize the extent of Hitler's expansionist goals. By 1939, though, it was no longer possible to quickly end Hitler's aggression. The Western leaders had waited too long. By the fall of that year, Hitler's German military was equal in power to that of Great Britain and France, and Hitler had already chosen his next target—Poland.

Throughout the spring and summer of 1939, Hitler began to clear the way for his march into Poland. Even as the French and British governments warned Hitler not to invade his eastern neighbor, they did little to prevent it. They even made plans to try to convince the Polish government to surrender some of its territory to Germany, just as the Czechs had been forced to do the previous year. Hitler went ahead with his plans, making gestures that were clearly designed to pave the way for a German invasion of Poland. In April, Hitler tore up the nonaggression pact Germany had with Poland, as well as a naval agreement with Great Britain that dated back to 1935. He then sent one of his top diplomats, Joachim von Ribbentrop, to the Soviet Union, where the German emissary hammered out two agreements with Stalin. One of these was a mutual economic agreement. The other, a nonaggression pact, stated that Germany and the Soviet Union would divide Poland between them but would not fight each other. As part of the pact, Hitler agreed to allow the Soviets to annex the Baltic countries and to wield considerable influence over Finland. In exchange, under a secret portion of the treaty, Stalin agreed to supply Germany with foodstuffs and raw materials for its industry, in exchange for manufactured goods.

In 1939, Soviet leader Joseph Stalin signed a controversial nonaggression pact with German dictator Adolf Hitler. The two leaders agreed to divide Poland between them and not to attack one another. The pact was negotiated by German diplomat Joachim von Ribbentrop (left, at back) and Stalin (at back, second from left).

The agreement between Germany and the Soviet Union placed the British and French in an awkward position. Historian Stephen Ambrose described the meaning of the new German-Soviet treaty:

The Nazi-Soviet pact stunned the world. One day Nazis and Communists were the bitterest enemies; the next they were allies. In a century full of political surprises, this was the greatest. Free from the threat of the Red Army, Hitler's demands for the return of the Polish Corridor increased. The French mobilized, sending their troops into [their] fortifications on their border with Germany. Britain also mobilized and finally began to re-arm, but gloom and disappointment swept London and Paris. Without the help of the United States and the Soviets, the British and French felt, rightly, that they could not match Germany's armed forces, the Wehrmacht.

With a handful of treaties that seemed to open the way to the east, Hitler ordered a German invasion of Poland to take place on September 1, 1939. The Germans invaded along two fronts, pushing hard and fast into Polish territory with their highly mechanized forces. The German army put into effect the so-called lightning war for which Hitler's military would become famous—*blitzkrieg*.

Although the Poles put up a spirited fight, their military was no match for the nine armored divisions the Germans unleashed against them. Five separate German armies, including a well-rounded combination of infantry, artillery, tank corps, and hundreds of Luftwaffe planes, attacked Poland. The Luftwaffe destroyed almost the entire Polish air force while most of its planes were still on the ground. Armed with only a handful of light tanks, its military centered in a dozen cavalry brigades, the conquest of Poland was completed in just 18 days. On September 27, the Polish capital was in the hands of the Wehrmacht (army). The next day, Stalin ordered the annexation of 77,000 square miles (123,920 kilometers) of eastern Poland. Hitler claimed the other half of Poland, turning it into a German protectorate.

Within two days of Hitler's invasion of Poland on the first day of September, France and Great Britain declared war on Germany. Even as they did so, they knew they faced fierce opposition from both Hitler's Germany and Stalin's Soviet Union. Hitler had accurately sized up the Western democracies before, and now he did not believe that his newly announced enemies would take any overt action against his forces immediately. He was right. During the six months after the Polish invasion—September 1939 to

April 1940—Great Britain and France avoided any direct assault on German troops. Instead, they organized a naval blockade. This period of "Phony War," as some critics of the strategy referred to it, gave Hitler time to invade Norway and Denmark, to Germany's north. Those attacks came on April 9, 1940. The invasion of Norway met little resistance. The Norwegian army was small and weak, and the blitzkrieg tactic allowed the Germans to capture strategic targets quickly, including large Norwegian munitions depots. The assault on the smaller nation of Denmark was carried out with even greater ease. Hitler would hold these two countries for the remainder of World War II.

Over the following months, Hitler's Wehrmacht managed what many people had considered impossible. Beginning on May 10, 1940, its blitzkrieg invasions were able to bring about the fall of Holland and Belgium. In desperation, the Dutch attempted to stop the German invasion by opening up their dikes and flooding their lands. Even this tactic failed. In the wake of the blistering attacks on the city of Rotterdam by the German Luftwaffe, Queen Wilhelmina fled the country, and the Dutch military surrendered.

Without missing a beat, the Germans moved on and invaded France. As the British Expeditionary Force and two French armies tried to stop the advance of Hitler's forces, they were completely routed (defeated). By late May, driven from their positions at Calais, France, British forces began to evacuate back to England. From May 27 through June 4, nearly half a million Allied troops, including 340,000 British troops and 120,000 French soldiers gathered at Dunkirk, France, and were carried across the English Channel in every available seacraft, including small fishing boats. Then, two weeks later, France fell under German occupation. Great Britain was left alone to stand against the brutality of the German war machine.

During the months that followed, Great Britain held

out against a seemingly endless series of aerial attacks by the German Luftwaffe. The German offensive, called Operation Sea Lion, began in mid-July 1940 and lasted for the next two months. Only the heroic efforts of the British Royal Air Force, which faced a superior number of German planes, managed to stave off the capitulation of the last Western power left after the German defeat of Denmark, Norway, Belgium, and France. Through sheer tenacity and defiance, by both the military and civilians, Great Britain prevented the German sea attack from taking place. As whole fleets of German ships waited for the signal to cross the icy waters of the North Atlantic and storm into Great Britain, the invasion date was reset three times before mid-September. Then, the extremely frustrated Hitler abandoned the idea of a full-scale invasion of the English island. From that point through the remainder of the war, Operation Sea Lion was officially placed on hold.

By the summer of 1940, the expanding war was being fought on a multitude of fronts, as the more powerful combatants jockeyed for control of strategic areas of European soil. Romania lost territory to Germany in late August, as German Foreign Minister Ribbentrop won large land cessions through negotiations with Romania's King Carol. By August, the Germans were moving in two directions simultaneously. They continued their aggressive fight to subdue Great Britain, while also advancing their claims across Eastern Europe. By the fall, Germany had been joined by Italy, as Mussolini's troops marched on Greece from their base in Albania. Although battered at home, the British, under the leadership of Prime Minister Winston Churchill, sent forces to aid the Greeks by early 1941. All major combatant parties—the Germans, the Soviets, and the British—understood the strategic importance of having control over large portions of Central and Eastern Europe as the war continued to escalate.

During that same summer, as Hitler's air force pounded England, Stalin was not sitting still. During June, he annexed the three Baltic States of Lithuania, Latvia, and Estonia, then seized Bessarabia, which had been under Romanian control. The Soviet assault on the Baltics was especially brutal. For a year after the June 1940 invasion, the Soviets shipped 130,000 native peoples from Latvia, Lithuania, and Estonia to work camps in Siberia (in northern Russia). Mass killings took place at the hands of Stalinist troops, including one outside the city of Smolensk in which 4,000 captives were shot in the back of the head, then buried in mass graves.

Once the Baltic countries were under Soviet control, Stalin ordered Finland, Russia's neighbor to the north, to surrender territory to provide a zone of defense in case Germany decided to attack Russia. When the Finnish government refused to give in to his demand to move the Russian border 25 miles (40 kilometers) into Finland, to help protect the Soviet city of Leningrad, Stalin ordered an attack. The advance of the Soviet Red army was slow and ineffective, however. Although the Soviet commander, Marshal Voroshilov promised Stalin he would have the Red army in the Finnish capital, Helsinki, in just one week, the campaign against the Finns actually stretched on from November 1940 until March 1941. By then, the Soviets had suffered through a successful, but tortuous advance. In his book *Ostfront: Hitler's War on Russia, 1941–45*, historian Charles Winchester noted the troubles the Soviets faced against the Finns:

> The Finns had fortified the Karelian isthmus [the main assault corridor used by the Russians] and the crude tactical methods adopted by the Red Army failed utterly. . . . Russian divisions struggled along the few roads to be cut off by Finnish ski troops. The 44th Rifle

Stalin's invasion of Finland was intended to be a way to take land to serve as a buffer against a German attack. The assault did not go well for the Soviets. Although the Soviet forces did achieve their goal, they sustained huge losses, including the dead soldiers seen here.

Division (rushed up from Kiev) was surrounded, broken into remnants unable to support each other, and annihilated. Newsreels showed roads chocked with tanks and equipment, frozen corpses of Russian soldiers clustered around them. Between the slaughter in the snow and the desperate frontal attacks, . . . the Red Army suffered some 200,000 casualties. Only weight of numbers enabled the Soviets to prevail.

In the spring of 1941, after Stalin's invasion of Finland, Hitler was preparing to shift to a new course of aggression in Europe. His list of targets and strategies would dramatically change the direction of the war during that fateful year. Hitler had clearly lost all hope of bringing about the rapid collapse of England. In Greece, as well as the Mediterranean Sea island of Crete, the German army was crushing the British forces sent to help the Greeks. By 1941, Hitler had determined the target of his next major offensive—the Soviet Union. First, however, he would have to pave the way.

Through that spring of 1941, Hitler forced weaker nations to sign agreements that would allow him to move German troops onto their soil without a fight. Finland signed a "transit agreement" that let the Wehrmacht march across Finnish lands to the east—toward Russia. Romania was also forced to grant Germany permission to send troops into Bulgaria, giving the Wehrmacht greater access to the Black Sea and the Soviet Union, while also hemming in Yugoslavia on all sides. In early April 1941, Hitler sent his forces against Yugoslavia. The attack caused the Yugoslav government to fall quickly. Before the end of the first day of the German invasion—April 6—the Yugoslav capital, Belgrade, had been destroyed by heavy bombing from the Luftwaffe. The Yugoslav air force was wiped out on the ground. In a repeat of the blitzkrieg that had already brought down much of Europe, German motorized infantry and Panzer tank divisions crushed all major resistance in Yugoslavia by mid-month. With the fall of Yugoslavia, Greece also collapsed under German control less than a week later.

Although such victories in Central, Southern, and Eastern Europe gave Germany a more strategic presence across the continent, they also managed to force the planned German offensive against the Soviet Union to be postponed. The invasion of Soviet soil was inevitable at this point, though. Hitler was becoming obsessed with the idea. The Winter War between the Soviets and the Finns had only strengthened Germany's resolve and confidence to attack Russia. The Soviets had not done well against the Finns. In fact, the war merely confirmed "the German High Command's perception of the Red Army [as] an old-fashioned ponderous mass just like the army Germany had defeated in World War I." Russian equipment had been lackluster and the infantry had fought poorly. To the Russians' further discredit, despite the military's weak performance against a much smaller Finnish force, the Soviet military command did almost nothing to correct the problems. Defeated Soviet generals were killed, purged for their failures to achieve victory under Stalin's orders. Such killings only robbed the Soviets of military leadership, however, since there were not enough top officers available to replace those exterminated.

Stalin did not appear, at least publicly, to fear a German invasion of his Soviet state. Incredibly, the Communist leader, despite the best advice of his top generals, including his new chief of general staff, Georgi Zhukov, actually "ordered the disarming of the fortifications along the Russian border." Stalin believed that his annexation of territory in Finland, the Baltics, Poland, and northern Romania had created an adequate zone of buffer states that would eliminate any possibility of a German invasion. Even if Hitler did turn on his alleged ally, Stalin was certain he would never reach the soil of Russia. Zhukov, certain the Germans would invade—and soon—tried in vain to convince Stalin of the dangers his military policies posed. The Soviet leader would not listen. It was a decision that would cost him and his people dearly.

War Engulfs
a Continent

Partly because of Stalin's faulty planning, the Soviet Union was not as prepared as it should have been when Hitler's attack finally came. As a result, the Soviets suffered many casualties. This badly wounded Russian soldier is being treated by the military medical staff.

After a year of planning, the German High Command stood poised to invade Russia, its leaders armed with an invasion plan, code-named Operation Barbarossa. Three plans had been developed, but the one selected set an assault on Leningrad, far to the north, as a first goal. German forces were to push hard, fast, and deep into Russian territory beginning in June. The Germans understood well the extent of the Soviet Union's military power. The Russian line of defense included 170 divisions divided into two large forces. Hitler had come to the conclusion that the Russian army was poorly led and inefficient, however. Such an army, reasoned the German dictator, could be beaten before the onset of winter.

The German High Command had placed nearly 3 million German troops, a total of 148 divisions, along the long stretch of territory known as the Russian frontier. This huge number of German forces consisted of four out of every five men in the entire German army! Two thousand Luftwaffe planes were also at the ready. Some of them had already flown reconnaissance missions over Soviet territory, snapping photographs of Russian military positions. German artillery was also in position—6,000 pieces in

New Weapons for a New War

As the Germans massed their forces in preparation to march into the Soviet Union, they had at their disposal new weapons designed for a new war. So did the Russians.

Whereas World War I had centered on infantry movements, horse-drawn artillery, and trench warfare, World War II brought to the field of battle new machines, tactics, and strategies that would change the face of battle. The Germans relied on a variety of tanks, especially the Panzer (German for "Panther"). The Panzer carried the best tank cannons of any used in the war, a whopping 88-millimeter (3.5-inch). Its imposing track and square-jawed look made the Panzer a formidable weapon, one that was highly durable in the field.

On the other side, the Russians relied heavily on one model of tank, the T-34. This tank was a military workhorse. It was patterned after an American design but was built in factories across the Soviet Union. The city of Stalingrad had a large factory, the Dzerhezinsky Tractor Works, that turned out T-34s rather than its usual tractors during the war. The T-34 weighed 32 tons (32,514 kilograms) and sported an 85-millimeter (3.4-inch) cannon, as well as two light machine guns. Its top speed was around 30 miles (48 kilometers) per hour and it had a range of 180 miles (290 kilometers). This armored weapon was designed with a depressed silhouette and its highly sloped, armored surfaces provided a limited target for enemy guns. The Soviet Union produced an amazing number of T-34s. Well over 50,000 of them were made through 1944. This fact caused Hitler to remark to one of his generals during the Russian campaign: "Had I known they had as many tanks as that, I would have thought twice before invading."

Performance was not always a question of how tanks were designed and all—prepared to flatten the enemy. The massed German force included 19 tank divisions—the Panzers—with 2,400 tanks at their disposal. An additional 14 divisions of highly mobile, motorized infantry were available and capable of moving with the speed of any Panzer division. The German troops were augmented by 14 Romanian divisions and 20 divisions of Finnish troops.

The Germans had planned their assault by dividing their invasion forces into three coordinated army groups.

built, but how they were put to use in the field. The Germans organized their tanks into ten Panzer divisions, with each division made up of about 300 tanks. These divisions were then subdivided into Panzer armies. Allied tanks, on the other hand, were organized into a handful of divisions, but most were sent out into separate battalions. In battle, German Panzer divisions would often mass together, bringing as many as 1,000 tanks into the same confrontation. The outnumbered Allied divisions were easily blown to bits. By organizing tank units to operate as one massive weapon in the field, the Germans were able to carry out their most effective strategy of the war—*blitzkrieg*.

As German armies moved with great efficiency on the ground, they also received support from the national air force, the Luftwaffe. Among the combat planes used by the Germans was the Junkers Ju87 Stuka. This dive bomber was first used against Communist forces in Spain in 1937. It had a top speed of 250 miles (402 kilometers) per hour and carried half-ton (508-kilogram) and 100-pound (45-kilogram) bombs. It was a terrifying sight on the battlefield as a Stuka approached in a nearly vertical dive, wailing a siren, then pulled out at the last possible minute.

Such weapons were essential to the strategies—both offensive and defensive—used by both the Germans and the Soviets during World War II. However, machines alone did not rule the battlefield. Despite the technological advances tanks and airplanes represented, as the German army marched across the Soviet Union in 1941, most of its supplies and cannons were hauled by the same source of power that had been used in warfare for centuries—the horse.

The Group North "was to advance from East Prussia, through the Baltic States and on to Leningrad." This group was under the command of Field Marshal Wilhelm von Leeb. The second army, Group Center, under General Fedor von Bock's command, was to march through the Pripet Marshes of northwestern Ukraine and Belarus, bound for strategic Soviet cities, including Minsk and Smolensk. The ultimate target of this German army, however, was the Russian capital—Moscow. Rounding out the German plan was Group South, with Field Marshal Gerd von Rundstedt in command. He was to lead his forces across southern Poland through Hungary and Romania. Then, von Rundstedt was to push hard across the open country of southern Russia, clear to the Ukraine. Here, across broad, open flat lands, the German Panzers would be able to move quickly.

Although Hitler's list of targets was lengthy, the Wehrmacht's primary goal was to inflict as many casualties on the Red army as possible. Although German armies and weaponry were superior to those of the Soviets, the attack could still fail if everything did not go according to plan. The Soviet Union was a gigantic nation. There was plenty of room for the Soviets to retreat in the face of an advancing German war machine. Historian Charles Winchester explained the purpose of the German invasion and the potential for failure:

> [The] German armies had not come to conquer cities. They were there to kill Russians. Hitler and the General Staff were in complete agreement, the Soviet forces had to be trapped and beaten in European Russia, preferably within 250 miles of the border. Their concern was that the Soviets might fall back deep into the Russian interior, drawing German forces into a battle of attrition on the edge of Asia.

Indeed, Stalin was alarmed by the increase of German armaments and troops along his border that spring, but chose to ignore it. He did not intend to fight the Nazis. Hitler was supposed to be his ally. Fighting the Germans would stretch Russian military capabilities to their limit. So, Stalin tried to avoid giving the Germans any reason to attack. In fact, since February 1940, the Soviets had shipped 1.5 million tons of grain to Germany, as well as 2 million tons of gasoline and other petroleum products and hundreds of thousands of tons of valuable ores and raw materials. Stalin wanted Hitler to know that his nation was a loyal supporter of the Nazi regime.

Despite Stalin's efforts, on June 22, the assault began. The Soviet army was almost completely unprepared, making Hitler even more certain of success. Many of Russia's fighting units were spread out across the vast Russian territory, taking part in summer exercises. Some were close to the invasion line when the Germans struck, but they were positioned so far forward that they could not be reinforced in time to turn the initial wave of Nazi aggression around. To make matters worse, if the Germans cut through Russia's first lines of defensive forces, the Soviets had practically no reserves to deal with massive numbers of Germans on Russian soil.

The German invasion was devastating. Air attacks pounded the Russian defense troops. When the Red air force took to the air, Nazi planes blew them out of the sky. In his book *Russia Besieged*, historian Nicholas Bethell wrote of that first day of German assault against the Soviets:

At approximately 3:00 A.M. "suddenly came a roar like thunder" as 6,000 German guns began bombarding Red Army defense posts, supply dumps and barracks all along the border. At the same time Luftwaffe aircraft swarmed out of the western sky, dropping their bombs on both military and civilian targets, but concentrating on airfields. By midday the Luftwaffe had knocked out 1,200 Russian warplanes—800 of them on the ground—while losing only 10 of its own. . . . German assault parties darted across bridges on foot or on motor-cycles, surprising Russian defenders before they could detonate demolition charges. . . . Russian border guards resisted valiantly, but nowhere did they manage to hold back the flood of German troops for long. . . . The sudden, massive blow shattered the Red Army.

During the following weeks and months, the Nazi war machine moved without mercy against the Russians. In just one week of fighting in July, the 4th Panzer group, with its tanks rolling across the Russian countryside, captured 300,000 Russian combatants and seized 2,500 tanks. As German tanks advanced on the Soviet city of Kiev, the Soviets attempted to stage a counteroffensive, but by the end of August, the Russian effort had failed and another 500,000 Russian soldiers had fallen into German hands.

By the first day of September, the German Group North, under the command of General Wilhelm von Leeb, had reached the outskirts of Leningrad. In an effort to save German manpower, however, the commander decided not to attack the city directly, but to lay siege to it instead. The Russians inside the city could not hold out forever, and food was already in short supply. During the first two weeks of September, German artillery shelled the city, cutting off the urban center from outside communication.

The city was not prepared for a siege. There was only one month's supply of food available, and most of that had to be rationed almost immediately. By October, desperation set in as thousands of Soviet people began to starve to death. In November alone, 11,000 residents died of hunger. For a while, small amounts of food were delivered across a nearby lake on barges, but by November 9, the Germans had cut off that access by having Luftwaffe dive bombers sink two dozen of the barges. By then, the lake had frozen over anyway, making barge traffic impossible. A frozen lake could still support Russian trucks, though, and by early December, small truck convoys crossed Lake Ladoga, to the east of Leningrad, to deliver limited amounts of supplies. The people ate anything they could get their hands on. After killing and consuming nearly every animal in the city, including pets, they turned to "[swallowing] hair oil and Vaseline; they made soup of dried glue from furniture joints and wallpaper." All outside efforts to feed the people of Leningrad were inadequate, and thousands continued to die from the lack of food.

As the Germans tightened the noose around Leningrad, other Nazi forces were busy elsewhere. With Kiev under German control, the Nazis turned to the northeast and prepared to attack Moscow, the Soviet capital. The German divisions sent to Moscow outnumbered Russian defensive forces by two to one. The Germans also enjoyed a similar ratio of tank strength. As for planes, the Germans had three Luftwaffe aircraft for every one the Soviets could put in the air.

The advance on Moscow began on September 30. Within three weeks, the Germans had already destroyed many of the Soviet troop units. By mid-October, two Soviet armies had been surrounded and overwhelmed, with a total of 650,000 men taken as prisoners. By October 20, the Germans were only 40 miles (64 kilometers) outside of Moscow. Stalin then ordered most of his government to evacuate the city and head east. He, however, along with his direct subordinates, determined to remain to defend the capital to the end. Only heavy October rain could slow the German troops. By the end of the month, the German advance had ground to a halt, as the Nazi forces faced a strong defense by the Russians as well as an endless bog of mud. Cold weather in November helped eliminate the mud, but forced the Germans to deal with the possibility of facing a brutal Russian winter.

Despite the Germans' difficulties, the Soviet army's strength had already been drastically reduced. As the winter snows began to fall, the Red army defending Moscow numbered just 800,000, with fewer than 800 tanks and about 350 planes. On each score, the Germans commanded greater numbers in each of these areas. Perhaps the only possible salvation for Moscow, other than severe winter weather, was the Red army commander whom Stalin had ordered to Moscow from Leningrad in early October, Marshal Georgi Konstantinovich Zhukov. Earlier in the fall, Zhukov had proven himself capable of handling the German blitzkrieg with dogged military skill and highly organized planning.

Sent to Leningrad by Stalin in mid-September, Zhukov's presence was crucial in responding to the German offensive. As soon as he arrived, Zhukov ordered a heavy bombardment of the Germans with artillery and mortars, along with air support to keep the Germans from breaching the outer defenses of the city at any point. This, along with the extensive maze of antitank trenches that the civilian population had dug, slowed the German Panzers to a crawl. Now, Zhukov was in Moscow, sent by Stalin to do his magic once again. Zhukov ordered antitank ditches to be dug around the city. A quarter of a million Moscow residents, called Muscovites, armed themselves with shovels and spades and began to dig furiously. Three out of four of the diggers were women. Zhukov then redeployed what troops were left in the city and brought in new field commanders, men he knew would stand and fight at all cost.

Zhukov's measures paid off. His tactics, along with the

Georgi Konstantinovich Zhukov was sent by Stalin to help the people of Leningrad defend themselves against the besieging German forces. Zhukov's skill at opposing siege warfare made him a heroic figure to the Soviet people.

increasingly harsh winter weather, reduced the Panzer divisions. By the end of November, one out of every three Panzers deployed against Moscow was no longer in service. German commanders began to worry about their lack of progress. According to Hitler's original plan, the Russians should have been defeated already. When asked by their superiors whether they felt they should push hard to try to defeat the defenders of the city or to set up winter camps and wait until spring, the German field commanders said they could go no farther.

Hitler had already made up his mind, however. He would accept no break in the offensive. He demanded that his forces press the battle. Throughout the final two weeks of November, the Germans moved against Moscow, organized in a "double envelopment of the Moscow defenses." Panzer units moved in from both the north and the south. For a while, Zhukov's defenses held fast. Then, on November 28, the 7th Panzer Division managed to cross the Volga Canal. Other units of German tanks also pushed past Russian defenses. By the end of the month, German Panzers were as close as 18 miles (29 kilometers) from the gates of Moscow.

Yet even as all seemed hopeless for the Muscovites defending the city, the Russian winter came on with a fury. Temperatures fell to -20°C (-4°F). Frostbite became the Germans' new enemy, as 100,000 men suffered from it, and it led to 2,000 amputations. One simple fact made military movement impossible for the Germans with the onset of winter: The German High Command had not sent its armies into Russia with winter clothing. To have done so would have given the appearance that the German offensive might not succeed before winter. The desperate German troops tried to line their thin uniforms with old newspapers to fight the cold. The Russian army, on the other hand, accustomed to the cold, continued to remain mobile and man their defenses. No German units advanced closer to the city after November 29. To the north, the German siege of Leningrad also ground to a halt.

Although the Wehrmacht had marched over thousands of square miles of Soviet territory during the last six months of 1941, the losses had been much greater than anyone, especially Hitler, had expected. By the end of November, the Germans had experienced nearly 750,000 casualties, including 200,000 dead. The Nazis had not lost so many troops in any earlier campaign. In the capture of Belgium, Holland, and France combined, the Germans had had 45,000 killed and 150,000 wounded. The Russian campaign had already brought many times that number of casualties, and the German losses continued to mount through the remaining winter months.

Then, in early December, the Russian army launched a counteroffensive against the German besiegers. New tanks from Great Britain arrived through an Arctic convoy. Reinforcements, including a Siberian force of ten divisions that Stalin had ordered to Moscow, bolstered the Soviet troops. These new defenders brought with them 1,000 tanks and an equal number of aircraft. On December 5, Zhukov ordered multiple Russian attacks against the German Panzer units. Over the next three weeks, the Soviets regained nearly all the territory the Germans had taken around Moscow since mid-November. Supplies began to reach Leningrad, averting the complete starvation of its defenders. By Christmas, having faced 100 hard-fighting Russian divisions, the German defenses collapsed. German troops were captured by the thousands, some "wearing women's furs and silk underclothing to supplement their inadequate uniforms against the cold." Even as the angry Adolf Hitler, from his headquarters in Germany, ordered the replacement of many of the generals he believed had failed him, one of them, Colonel General Franz Halder, put the new reality of the war into perspective when he wrote: "The myth of invincibility of the German Army was broken."

The Russians understood that they held a stronger position during the winter months than they had during the last eight months of fighting. For the rest of the bitter winter, there was little fighting on the Russian front. During January, the Germans pushed slightly against the perimeter line that had been established the previous month by Zhukov's counteroffensive, but little changed as a result. Many people, including the Germans, believed that the possibility of an all-out defeat of the Soviets had already been lost. Still, Hitler kept his men in the field, where they were ordered to wait until spring.

The German army had already suffered 1.3 million casualties in the war. The army surrounding Moscow accumulated another 55,000 dead and 100,000 wounded in December and January alone. By January, three out of every four German tanks sent into the campaign against Moscow had been destroyed. More than 2,000 Luftwaffe planes had been ruined completely and another 1,400 lay damaged, unable to fly without additional repairs and maintenance.

The Soviets had faced staggering losses, too. Of the 22,000 tanks the Soviets had in service before 1939, only 1,000 were still operational. Every mechanized Soviet corps had been destroyed. A total of 177 Soviet rifle divisions no longer existed. In the defense of Moscow, where the fighting had been extremely intense, Stalin's forces had counted one million casualties. Surrendering Soviet armies had given the Germans 3 million prisoners of war. In the midst of the winter of 1941–1942, the Russians could muster only about 250,000 troops to maintain the defense of their Communist nation.

Despite the losses on both sides, the Germans and the Soviets knew that more fighting lay ahead. Looking forward to May, the German High Command organized more than 20 new divisions and sent them to Russia. German women, whom Hitler had refused to put into military service earlier in the war, were now allowed to take work as clerks and drivers. This freed up more

German men for military duty. As a result of these efforts, the German army received 900,000 new recruits during the winter of 1941–1942. Even so, the number of German troops ready for action by May of 1942 remained fewer than the number that had invaded the Soviet Union during the previous summer. Officially, German divisions were considered to be at full strength. In reality, losses in the field had reduced the numbers of some divisions by as much as one-third.

As for the Russians, they did not waste the months during which the Germans were at a standstill outside their major cities. Additional recruits were tapped as Soviet military planners worked furiously to increase the number of Red army troops to 9 million. Dozens of new divisions were formed, and Soviet factory workers in the east cranked out nearly 5,000 new tanks, 14,000 artillery pieces, 50,000 mortars, and 3,000 planes. Historian Charles Winchester described the tremendous efforts the Soviets made to salvage their much-needed industrial capacity:

Behind the Russian lines men and women were struggling to survive too. In sub-zero temperatures, sometimes in near-total darkness, they unloaded machine tools from rail cars and reassembled whole factories in remote areas. The success with which Soviet industry was evacuated east in 1941 was justly celebrated by the USSR as a triumph as significant as any victory on the battlefield. . . . Iron, steel and engineering plants were shipped to the Urals, Siberia or Kazakhstan. . . and sixteen million people went with them, laboring with grim determination to get the machines turning again. The Yak fighter factory in Moscow was dismantled and shipped to Siberia where production resumed after just six days on site. In three months production exceeded the quotas achieved in Moscow.

Stalin, who had hundreds of thousands of German soldiers still on his soil, knew that the spring and summer of 1942 would probably decide the fate of his nation and of its people. As Stalin made military plans for the spring, he guessed that the Germans would concentrate at hitting Moscow with all their strength. He was wrong.

Meanwhile, Adolf Hitler was busy making plans of his own. Although his troops had not succeeded in bringing about the defeat of the Soviet Union by the end of 1941, Hitler was not prepared to scale back his ultimate goal. Instead, he would change the timeline and the direction of the German offensive in 1942. Historian Stephen Ambrose described Hitler's strategy:

> . . . Hitler's plans for his 1942 summer offensive were ambitious enough: hold fast on the central front, capture Leningrad in the north, and make the main assault in the south, where Stalingrad would be captured or bombed into ruins, while other German forces would move on to seize the Caucasus, with its rich oil fields. . . . The German offensive opened in early June [1941], and at first it looked like the old story of blitzkrieg advances through bewildered Soviet defenders. But Hitler . . . now decided to capture both Stalingrad and the Caucasus at the same time. . . . [He] was about to blunder the German Army into a catastrophe.

Hitler's well-oiled war machines had stormed into the Soviet Union with speed and precision. With the lengthy winter, however, the German army's supply of fuel had dwindled dramatically. As the German leader planned his 1942 campaign, the oil shortage led him to order the main German assault to take place in southern Russia, toward the oil-rich region of the Caucasus Mountains, between the Black Sea and the Caspian Sea.

Hitler issued his plan with orders for the German military on April 5. The assault plan included multiple field movements. In the Crimean region, Hitler's 11th army was to attack a Russian army on the Kerch peninsula, then capture the city of Sevastopol on the Black Sea. One part of his plan compelled Hitler to divide Group South into two armies, Group A and Group B. Group A was to move directly for the Caucasus in April, while Group B would drive south to the Don River. This would place Hitler's troops within bombing distance of another major Russian urban center, "Stalin's City"—Stalingrad.

Hitler Plots His Strategy

Despite their weak response to the initial German attack, the Soviet troops responded with a fierce counteroffensive in the spring of 1942. Among the Soviet forces were units of automatic riflemen like these.

he first fighting between the Soviets and the Germans in the spring of 1942 began not with a German attack, but a Russian one. On May 12, a Soviet army under the command of Marshal Semion Timoshenko, attempted to rout the German 6 and 17 armies from their positions at key crossing places along the Dnieper River in the Ukraine. Despite some initial advancement, the Soviets were crushed, and two of their tank corps were annihilated. Three Soviet armies—the 6th, 9th, and 57th—were pulverized. The Germans had rolled over the Russians, destroying "twenty infantry and seven cavalry divisions, and 13 armored brigades . . . losing 214,000 prisoners, 1,246 tanks, and 2,026 guns." The commander of the Russian 6th army, Lieutenant-General A. M. Gorodnyansky was killed during the bloody engagement, and his fellow commander, Lieutenant-General K. P. Podlas, committed suicide along with his entire staff rather than be taken alive. Soviet losses after less than two weeks of fighting came to nearly a quarter of a million men.

During those same days of battle, the Soviets lost control of their positions elsewhere, including on the Crimean front. Russian forts, built in the form of huge concrete and steel barricades, were leveled by the Germans, who used huge siege cannons that moved along rail lines on flatcars. The immense guns included a 24-inch (61-centimeter) mortar named "Karl" and a 31-inch (79-centimeter) railway cannon, known as "Gustav." The Gustav's barrel was 100 feet (31 meters) long and weighed 130 tons (132,086 kilograms). This power weapon, referred to as "the biggest gun ever built," fired "7-ton armor-piercing shells [that] destroyed a Soviet ammunition bunker under Severnaya Bay, passing through the water and 100-foot of rock before detonating inside the magazine." This gigantic weapon could be fired three times an hour.

At the same time that the German Luftwaffe destroyed Soviet air regiments, Russian land forces lost 350 tanks, 3,500 artillery pieces, and accumulated a staggering list of 175,000 casualties. When the Germans occupied the Crimean city of Sevastopol, home to 30,000 people, on July 3, two out of every three of the city's residents were either deported to work camps or killed. Ninety thousand Red army troops were captured.

A jubilant Hitler excitedly moved his headquarters to the Ukrainian city of Vinnitsa so he could be closer to the fighting inside the Soviet Union. The Nazi leader had become single-minded that summer as he carried out his second campaign against the Soviets. Although German armies were still fighting in many other places around the globe, including North Africa, the Mediterranean Sea, the Atlantic, Hitler's entire focus seemed to center on the advances his forces were preparing to make in the Soviet Union. Historian Charles Winchester described the German dictator's focus:

> That he would continue to concentrate on the Russian front . . . demonstrates its overriding importance to him. It also exposes the limits of his horizons. In what was now a world war involving four continents, Hitler remained obsessed with the Eastern front and would attempt to micro-manage the campaign there, while critical events in other theaters passed him by.

As the Germans began to push their way across the southern region of the Soviet Union that summer, they had many targets on which to focus. At center stage were the Soviet oil fields of the Caucasus. When the Germans took the fields, the Nazis would have limitless fuel, and would prevent the Russians from using it.

With the great battle between the Nazi forces of Germany and the Communist fighters of Stalin ready to commence in earnest by late June, the numbers of troops positioned on both sides were staggering. Although the German troops were reduced to half of their original invasion force from 1941, they had forced some one million fighters from Romania, Hungary, and Italy to fight with them. Perhaps a total of 3.25 million soldiers under German orders were committed to the fight on Soviet soil. In comparison, the Red army may have numbered a total of 5 million men. This difference in the size of the two armies became crucial as the 1942 campaign was waged. The Soviets, who already had more troops, were able to create new units from a vast reserve of manpower. The Germans, however, had no other troops at their disposal. This fact alone would cost the Germans' efforts dearly over the long run.

With their success at Sevastopol, the forces of the German 11th army were free to launch toward their next objectives, the Caucasus and Stalingrad. The plan concocted by Hitler and his High Command had called for Group B to fight its way to the wide bend of the Don River, then proceed toward Stalingrad and the Caucasus. Meanwhile, Group A, made up of the 1st Panzer army, the 17th army, and the 3rd Romanian army, was to march on the city of Rostov, 200 miles (322 kilometers) southwest of Stalingrad. Once Group A occupied Rostov, that force was to turn east, join Group B, and push the Red army back to Stalingrad and the Volga, killing as many Soviets as possible in the process. With the Soviet army in the region decimated, the Germans could then turn again to the southeast and take control of the Caucasus and its oil.

For a time, everything seemed to go according to the German plan. On June 28, the German 4th Panzer hit a Russian railroad junction near the town of Voronezh, on the Volga River, 200 miles (322 kilometers) northwest of Stalingrad. By June 30, the German 6th army, under the command of Friedrich von Paulus encountered, Russian troops who had abandoned their field in a chaotic retreat. Then, unexpectedly, the 4th army ran into trouble. Capturing Voronezh had not been part of Hitler's original plan. When the urban center's outskirts fell easily under the control of German tanks, Group B's Field Marshal Fedor von Bock asked Hitler for permission to occupy the city. Surprisingly, Hitler left the decision to the commander. Bock ordered two divisions of Panzers to Voronezh. Only when the Germans became embroiled in desperate street fighting as the Russians hurriedly sent reinforcements into the city, did Hitler realize the mistake that had been made in trying to take Voronezh. With Bock bottled up in the city, Red army troops by the thousands were moving out of harm's way, slipping south toward the Caucasus.

Then, Hitler made some poor military decisions of his own. Certain that he had the Red army on the run, he decided to change his field plans. He split Group A and Group B again. He ordered Group A toward the Caucasus, and gave instructions to Group B to move directly toward the city of Stalingrad. Hitler's change in strategy was even more foolhardy than it appeared. Before sending Group B on its new mission, he split off the 4th Panzer army and sent it to join Group A. This reduced Group B's number of troops and left its one remaining unit, the 6th army, under the command of Field Marshal Friedrich von Paulus with no other direct support. Now the 6th army faced even greater odds as it marched deep in Soviet territory. Without the 4th Panzer, Paulus's forces would have a more difficult time breaching any serious Russian resistance in defense of Stalingrad. If he did not have enough armored vehicles at his disposal, the German commander would have to make a direct frontal assault, rather than surround the city as had been done the previous year at Moscow and Leningrad.

Hitler's change of plans and the separation of the 4th Panzer from Paulus's undefeated 6th army did not sit well with his military commanders. As historian William Craig explained, many of his officers

> could not believe the Fuhrer [Hitler] would commit such a blunder. . . . When Hitler pivoted an entire army across another's path, he had defied the military maxim that any interference with the delicate internal functions of a massed body of troops frequently leads to chaos. And on the steppe roads of Russia, the Sixth Army stopped dead while swarms of vehicles and men from the Fourth Panzer Army cut left to right across its line of advance. Enormous traffic jams developed. Tanks of one army mingled with those of the other; supply trucks got lost in a maze of contradictory signposts and directions handed out by irate military policemen. Worse, the Fourth Army took the bulk of the oil and gasoline meant to fuel both armies.

Paulus, in particular, was angry, since he knew that any delay in his advance on Stalingrad would only allow the Russians to establish stronger defenses.

Next, Hitler followed up his reassignment of the 4th Panzer with additional changes in the placement of German troops inside the Soviet Union. He sent five divisions under the command of Field Marshal Erich von Manstein away from the Crimean region, north to Leningrad. This move took away yet another German force that would be needed to ensure victory in the Caucasus. Then, Hitler removed two of his best tank divisions from southern Russia and ordered them to advance toward France. (Hitler was concerned that the Allies might set up a second European front in France that year.)

Stalin's Secret Weapon: A Spy Named "Lucy"

As Hitler planned his assault on various Soviet targets for the summer of 1942, the Soviet premier, Joseph Stalin, kept informed about the details of the German plan through contacts within Hitler's own inner circle of generals. The efforts of an extremely successful spy ring helped Stalin gain knowledge about German strategies.

Stalin's spies, located across Europe, fed him huge amounts of information during the war. Before the German invasion of the Soviet Union in the summer of 1941, Stalin's agents had told him of the German plan. He ignored their warnings, certain that such intelligence could not be true. Only after the Germans smashed across the Russian border in June 1941, did the Soviet leader take his field agents more seriously.

Several spy systems were serving the Soviet cause even before the war began. One unit was centered in Paris. It was led by an agent named Leonard Trepper, code-named "Big Chief." Trepper was a Polish Jew who made contacts with various German officials, military attachés, and businessmen, some of whom provided him with information on German military plans. Another agent, a Hungarian named Alexander Rado, worked out of Switzerland, where German authorities could not reach him. One of his field operatives was Rudolf Rossler, a shadowy figure known by his code name, "Lucy."

Rossler was a small, shy, unassuming man who wore eyeglasses and

At that moment, German Group A, deep in the Caucasus, was facing a spirited defense put up by the Russians. Already, Group A was in terrible need of reinforcements—which Hitler had just sent to France. Despite the odds stacked against the German forces, when Group A Field Marshal Sigmund Wilhelm List seemed to be making little headway against the Soviets in the Caucasus, Hitler sacked him.

Hitler's changes in his operation plans had upset almost every part of his overall offensive efforts. Only through the determination of some of Hitler's commanders did the German dictator finally reconsider his redeployment of the 4th Panzer army. Near the end of July, he issued new orders yet again, this time sending the 4th Panzer, back to the north, where it would meet up again with Paulus's 6th army.

hardly looked like a secret agent. As "Lucy," he had ties to figures within the Germany Army High Command itself. He maintained his sources with such secrecy that they remain unnamed even today. It was through Rossler that the Soviet leadership, especially Stalin, knew about nearly every important decision Hitler made, usually within 24 hours!

When the Russian campaign was on the drawing table, Stalin knew its details, including how many and which divisions would be used and the "operation's ultimate goal of severing the Volga river lifeline and capturing the oil fields of the Caucasus." This allowed Stalin to shift his troops to meet the German forces. Even as the German offensive during the summer of 1942 unfolded, Rossler continued to feed Stalin information, including the major changes Hitler made in the middle of July when he shifted the 4th Panzer group away from the 6th army.

Sometimes, what "Lucy" told him seemed too unbelievable to Stalin, and he hesitated to follow up on it. The changes Hitler made at Voronezh are one example. Even as the Germans headed for Stalingrad, Stalin was certain that the ultimate goal of the German offensive was to capture Moscow, not the city on the Volga. When field reports confirmed the accuracy of Rossler's intelligence reports, however, Stalin responded with confidence in what "Lucy" told him.

The weak leadership of German officer Friedrich von Paulus helped cause the failure of the Nazi troops to defeat the Soviets early in the campaign against Stalingrad. Paulus was a cautious leader whose delays lost precious opportunities for the German forces.

"So many precious days have been lost," fumed one of Hitler's generals. On August 5, though, Hitler and his generals received some encouraging news from the Stalingrad front. The 6th army was in position to "close on two enemy armies." Meanwhile, the 4th Panzer army had captured an important railroad center just 73 miles (118 kilometers) southwest of Stalingrad.

As the German armies neared the city of Stalingrad, the Russian defenders had taken advantage of the slow, confused German approach. Half a million Soviets were in the city and the surrounding suburban countryside. All of them were prepared to protect their city and their homeland. The defense perimeters were generally manned by Soviet soldiers, but the people of Stalingrad, including women and young men, had been armed and were ordered to defend the city from within.

Stalin understood what had been lost already as the Germans prepared to march on the city that had been named after him. He received reports that summer of flagging Russian morale. When Soviet forces fell back and retreated from the city of Rostov in the face of advancing German Panzers, the blow was severe.

Back in early July, Stalin had not considered the possibility of having to defend Stalingrad against a siege laid by the Germans. He expected that the Wehrmacht was bound for the Caucasus oil fields, and that cities such as Stalingrad were nothing more than side goals. In mid-July, Stalin had approved a plan to remove Red army forces to the east as far as the Volga, intending to force the Nazis to meet them on the open plains of a windswept Russia. When Hitler divided the 4th Panzer from the 6th army, however, and sent the latter toward Stalingrad, Stalin reworked his plan. He now believed a stand at Stalingrad was inevitable.

Stalin informed the city council to make preparations for the defense of Stalingrad. By July 21, the city fathers were to have every man, woman, and child working to establish a fortification complex around Stalingrad, including antitank ditches. Then, one week later, Stalin issued an important directive to every Red army unit in the field. Stalin's Order 227 commanded an endless stand against the Germans. No one was to shirk his or her responsibility. In the directive, Stalin summed up the situation that he and his fellow Soviets faced in the late summer of 1942:

We have lost 70 million inhabitants and an annual production of 13 million tons of grain and 10 million tons of metal. We have now lost our superiority in reserves of manpower. . . . To continue to retreat is to give up ourselves and our country for lost. Every inch of territory we concede strengthens the enemy and weakens the defense of our country. We must oppose pitilessly the view that we can retreat indefinitely because our country is rich and large, our population immense, and our grain always abundant. Such statements are untrue and harmful; they weaken us and strengthen the enemy. . . . Every position and every yard of Soviet territory must be defended tenaciously and to the last drop of our blood.

The order included a stirring phrase—"*Ni Shagu Nazad!*"—"Not another step back!"

To reinforce his order and its sentiment, Stalin ordered that 13,500 of his own troops be executed, in order to remove troublemakers, shirkers, and people Stalin deemed less than zealous in their patriotism. His harsh discipline condemned others to serve in special military units called "*Strafbats,*" which were prisoner battalions. These condemned Soviet troops were sometimes placed in front-line assault positions to bear the brunt of a German attack. Others were sent across open fields where enemy mines were suspected to be. These kinds of orders typically resulted in the deaths of these prisoners who were considered traitors to the Soviet cause.

By July 30, the 4th Panzer had reunited with Paulus's 6th army, restoring some of the lost power of Group B. Just five days later, the 6th army had advanced to Kalatsch, on the Don River, just 30 miles (48 kilometers) due west of Stalingrad. A Russian force, the 1st tank army, put up a tough resistance against the Germans, slowing their progress by a week. Only when Paulus maneuvered his tanks into a pincer movement did the fighting near Kalatsch bring him victory. During the next two weeks, Paulus was joined by two tank corps, the 14th Panzer, under the command of General G. von Wietersheim and the 24th Panzer.

It was now August, near the end of a fighting season, when good weather would soon come at a premium. The Germans were advancing daily. They were facing resistance, but were still managing to achieve victories with minimal casualties. The Soviets were adding to their numbers, however, even as they pulled back from their advance positions. On July 23, the Russians had 16 reserve divisions near the long, arcing bend in the Don River region west of Stalingrad. By July 30, another 28 divisions had joined them. Three weeks later, in late August, there were 60 Red army divisions, and an additional 13 would soon arrive.

This fact alone—the ability to find reinforcements whenever they were needed—had always been the advantage the Soviets enjoyed as they faced the Germans on their own soil. Stalin had nearly unlimited reserves of troops. The Germans, on the other hand, had to move across open Russian steppe country with only the troops they had originally brought on the campaign. This potential problem had been clear to the German High Command from the start, and Hitler himself had been reminded about it long before he sent his forces across Russia in the summer of 1942. When an officer made a report informing Hitler "that still in 1942 Stalin would be able to muster from one to one-and-a-quarter million fresh troops in the region north of Stalingrad and west of the Volga, not to mention half a million men in the Caucasus, Hitler flew at the man who was reading with clenched fits and foam in the corners of his mouth and forbade him to read any more such idiotic twaddle." The German dictator wanted to hear of nothing but victories for his troops in the Soviet Union, and through August 1942, this was possible. The Germans were moving closer to Stalingrad with each passing day.

Meanwhile, in the city on the Volga, the defenses were in place. The people of Stalingrad waited impatiently, anxious to hear any news about the action to the west.

The City
on the Volga

Stalingrad was a center of industry within the Soviet Union. Among its most important businesses was the Dzerhezinsky Tractor Works, seen here finishing the first tractors it produced. During World War II, the tractor plant would change its operations to make military equipment instead of tractors.

T he city of Stalingrad, positioned along the meandering west bank of the Volga River, the mother of all Russian waterways, had not been on Hitler's original list of Soviet cities to capture when he first sent his troops onto Russian soil in the summer of 1941. By the summer of 1942, however, after a frustrating year for the Germans and a harrowing one for the Soviets, Stalingrad had become the target in which Hitler was most interested. The city was an ancient one, a site of early Mongol occupation. It had also seen earlier invasions, including one in 1237 at the hands of Kublai Khan, the grandson of Genghis Khan, ruler of the Mongolian Empire. For hundreds of years, the region had served as a border post for Russian soldiers who used the site as a springboard for assaults on Mongolian outposts to the east. By the late 1500s, the Russian czar founded a trading outpost along the Volga called *Tsaritsyn*, a Tartar word that translated as "yellow water."

Tsaritsyn was a crossroads for war. Russian bands of highwaymen and river pirates attacked unarmed people constantly as the outpost community remained an important stop along trade routes connecting Europe to Asia. In 1670, a warrior named Stenka Razin captured the Russian city after a violent siege. A century later, Yemelyan Pugachev led a revolt at Tsaritsyn in an attempt to free the local Russian peasants. He failed, and Czarina Catherine the Great had his head chopped off.

By the nineteenth century, the city had begun to feel the impact of the expanding European Industrial Revolution. Because Russia was still a poor region of Europe, it welcomed foreign investment. In 1875, a French company organized and built the first steel mill in the Volga region where Tsaritsyn was located. The city experienced additional growth and expansion, and was soon home to more than 100,000 people. Other factories and industrial plants followed, and by World War I, Tsaritsyn was one of the most industrialized cities, for its size, in all of Russia. One out of every four residents of the city worked in an industry-related job. Yet the city was still primitive by twentieth-century standards. In his book *Enemy at the Gates*, historian William Craig described the city following World War I:

> Despite the boom, the city reminded visitors of America's wild west. Clusters of tents and ramshackle houses sprawled aimlessly along the riverbank; more than four hundred saloons and brothels catered to a boisterous clientele. Oxen and camels shared the

unpaved streets with sleek horse-drawn carriages. Cholera epidemics scourged the population regularly as the result of mountains of garbage and sewage that collected in convenient gullies.

The people of Tsaritsyn also witnessed the events of the Russian Revolution. For some time, the city was the center of a military struggle between the Communists and the White army, as they struggled for control of the revolution and the future of Russia. Joseph Stalin fought off several White army assaults from Tsaritsyn until he won a final victory in 1920. The people of the Volga community renamed their city Stalingrad, in honor of the Communist leader. Stalin invested greatly in the industrial future of his namesake city, establishing new factories that produced everything from chemicals to weapons to tractors. By the beginning of World War II, Stalingrad had become home to 500,000 people.

The Stalingrad that lay waiting for the German attack in the summer of 1942 "looked like a giant caterpillar, sixteen miles long and filled with smokestacks belching forth clouds of soot that told of its value to the Soviet war effort." Most of the larger industrial plants — including the Barrikady Gun Factory, the Lazur Chemical Plant, the Red October plant (a foundry and machine-tool complex), and the Dzerhezinsky Tractor Works, a factory of gigantic proportions — were located at the northern end of the city. These industrial power-houses made Stalingrad strategically important to both the Soviets and the Germans.

The Lazur Chemical Plant, a yellow brick complex, spanned an entire city block. A train line ran around the factory in a gigantic oval. To its north, the Red October plant, "a maze of foundries and calibration shops" produced small arms and metal parts for manufacturing.

Continuing north, the Barrikady Gun Factory stretched along a quarter mile of the Volga. There, workers assembled large weapons, including heavy-caliber gun barrels. Rounding out the northern most sector of Stalingrad's industrial district, the Dzerhezinsky Tractor Works stood as a potent symbol of both the Communist-led economy of the 1930s and the Soviet war effort of the 1940s. Built just ten years earlier, the plant had produced thousands of tractors and other farm machinery. The main factory was a mile-long (1.6-kilometer-long) building. It was so large that it contained 10 miles (16 kilometers) of railroad lines under its enormous glass roof. At the start of World War II, the plant had been retooled to become the largest manufacturer of the Red army's T-34 tank.

Shadowing the entire industrial complex of Stalingrad's northern sectors were massive worker apartment buildings, 300 of them. Each multistory complex provided homes for hundreds, even thousands, of workers. A beehive of urban attractions — movie houses, playgrounds, groceries, parks, schools, even a local circus — were all within easy reach of the apartment buildings. The entire urban community — the housing, shops, amusements, parks, and, of course, the factories — had been built by the Communist government. For Stalin, these centers of worker productivity were his showplace to the outside world, grand symbols of the efficiency of the Communist state. Since Stalingrad was a port community, the Volga was the community's lifeline to the outside world. On one bank of the river, hundreds of boats, including shipping barges and steamers, were lined up in tight formation. On the opposite bank lay long, flat plains. As the invading Germans advanced from the west, rescue and reinforcements for the worried Soviets of Stalingrad would come from the east, across the Volga.

At the south end of Stalingrad was the downtown residential, business, and government district. This section of the city was less industrial. Here, was the greatest concentration of storefronts and businesses, offices and homes, including single-story wooden houses and large apartment dwellings. In this hub of the city stood Railroad Station Number One. For months prior to the battle, trains had brought thousands of Soviet people, many fleeing from other beleaguered Russian cities, including Leningrad, Odessa, and Moscow, to Stalingrad.

Near the train station stood Red Square, which included government buildings, the local offices of the Communist newspaper, *Pravda*, and the central post office. *Pravda* published informational pieces for the local people as the German attack neared, including articles on how to respond during an air raid and how to ration food. The news *Pravda* carried about the fighting between the Red army and the Germans usually played down Soviet losses.

Other buildings in the central part of the city included a library and a theater, the Gorki, where "a philharmonic orchestra . . . played regularly in an ornate auditorium festooned with graceful crystal chandeliers hovering over a thousand velvet-backed seats." There was a public garden, a bank, a flour mill, shops, and the greatest store in the city, Univermag Department Store, located on the northeastern part of Red Square. Most of the store's inventory was depleted by the end of the summer of 1942. Only essential clothing items such as "underwear, socks, trousers, shirts, coats, and boots" were left. Aside from these typical urban buildings, the streets of Stalingrad offered an urban maze of brick, mortar, stone, and wood, which would soon be reduced to absolute rubble in the face of the coming German attack.

In the part of the city that divided the southern business district from the industrial north end was a natural rise in the landscape, known locally as Mamaev Hill. To the people of Stalingrad, it was a popular picnic ground, although hundreds of years earlier it had served as a Tartar burial ground. Mamaev was a sloping, grassy rise of 336 feet (102 meters), and, from its top, a viewer could scan the entire city, taking in a grand view of both a sprawling urban landscape and the meandering waters of the Volga. As historian William Craig described it, "To the west, there was an uninhabited stretch of steppe country, badly broken by . . . deep, dried-up riverbeds." Just north of the hill's base was the Lazur Chemical Plant.

In the first week of August 1942, Field Marshal Paulus ordered his forces to continue their advance toward Stalingrad. By August 7, Luftwaffe planes were bombing the small town of Ostrov, 20 miles (32 kilometers) west of the Don River and about 60 miles (97 kilometers) from Stalingrad. Ostrov was the last Russian defensive outpost west of the Don. There, German planes destroyed the Russian 62nd army headquarters. Before the day was over, the German 6th Army had captured 57,000 Soviets and destroyed more than 1,000 tanks. Paulus was jubilant. He delivered a message to his men: "Thanks to the brave advance . . . the possibility of this victory was set. . . . We proudly think of the fallen . . . on to the next task set by the Fuhrer [Hitler]."

As the German 6th army advanced toward the Don River, another Wehrmacht force, the 4th Panzer army, under the command of General Hermann Hoth, was moving northeast toward the Volga. As the 4th Panzer and the 6th army pushed against Red army resistance, units of the Soviet military abandoned their outposts and field positions across the hill country outside Stalingrad

A German Panzer division crossing the Don River in Russia during World War II, in anticipation of advancing on Stalingrad.

and escaped into the city. The Germans pushed on, slowly but deliberately.

As several German armies approached the Russian city on the Volga, they were part of a large-scale operation. Swinging in wide arcs, the Wehrmacht forces were strung out along a seemingly endless line. In his book *The Secret of Stalingrad*, historian Walter Kerr described the scope of the German movements: "In contrast to Waterloo (1815), where the field was a mile or two wide, or Gettysburg (1863), where it was never more than three, the struggle for the approaches to Stalingrad and the Caucasus was waged on a three-hundred-mile

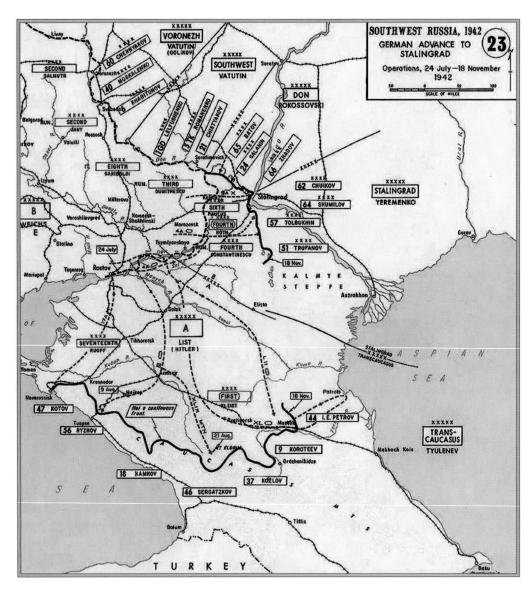

A map of the German advance on Stalingrad during the period July 1942 through November 1942.

front." Paulus's forces in the 6th army alone, as they moved toward their urban target, numbered 225,000 men, and were backed by 7,000 artillery pieces and 500 tanks.

Even as Paulus ordered his men forward, he was cautious, taking care not to thrust too far ahead without support, for fear of a Soviet trap. Thus, "he inched his way forward like a mouse feeling for cheese." His advance scouts saw little ahead to cause any concern, as they passed fields manned by Russian peasants.

For both the advancing Germans and the Soviets lying in defensive positions on the outskirts of Stalingrad, the summer was hot and dry. As the Germans moved, thousands of men and machines stirred up thick clouds of yellowish dust. The soldiers' uniforms were covered with it.

Under the hot August sun, the Germans continued toward Stalingrad. Russian troops south of Stalingrad faced strong German attacks early in the month. This portion of the Russian defensive line was under the command of Red Army General Rodion Malinovsky. It did not have enough troops to meet the heavy German assault. Wehrmacht army Group A, with assistance from Hoth's 4th Panzer group, rolled Malinovsky's men back, sending them racing toward Stalingrad. With an open road before him, Hoth received orders from the German High Command to turn left and head straight for the heart of Stalingrad.

The Russians moved quickly to meet this new threat, though. Regrouping their forces, including the Soviet 64th army and the 57th army, the Soviets fought hard and "stopped Hoth and drove him back in the first German defeat since the opening of the summer campaign." The Russians took some comfort in the victory, and they realized, just as the German commanders did, exactly what kind of problems the Wehrmacht was going to face in the weeks ahead. As Walter Kerr put it, "The closer the enemy got to Stalingrad, the less room he had for maneuver; and the farther he got from his base of supplies, the more he suffered from a shortage of fuel and ammunition."

Paulus continued to push his 6th army forward despite such increasing limits on its flexibility. During the first days of August, the Russian 1st tank army

A Visit From Churchill

In the midst of the German assault on Stalingrad during August 1942, Stalin received a special guest—the prime minister of Great Britain, Winston Churchill. The two leaders met in Moscow, in a prearranged secret meeting. They had a lot to talk about.

At the center of their meeting was one major looming issue: the question of when the Soviet Union's allies, the United States and Great Britain, would establish a second major war front in Western Europe. Doing so would force the Germans to fight on two significant fronts in Europe alone, not to mention other regions, such as the Mediterranean and North Africa. Stalin was extremely impatient for Churchill and the U.S. president, Franklin Roosevelt, to start such a front to help relieve Stalin's forces as they faced hundreds of thousands of German troops on their own soil.

Churchill attended the meeting with no intention of promising Stalin such a front any time soon, however. In fact, the British leader went to Moscow knowing that the Western Allies did not intend to establish a new front in 1942, or even in 1943. Although Franklin Roosevelt and many leaders in the U.S. military were prepared to open a Western European front soon, Churchill was opposed to it. In his book *The Peoples of the British Isles*, historian Thomas Heyck described the standoff between the Soviets and Churchill:

> The Russians naturally wanted the Western Allies to open a second front in France as soon as possible, in order to drain off some of the terrible German pressure on Soviet troops. The Americans . . . wanted to open a second front by means of a cross-channel invasion. . . . Churchill and his generals, however, remembered the awful bloodletting of the First World War and Dunkirk as well. They preferred to attack on the periphery of Europe . . . in Italy or the Balkans.

crossed the Don River and fought hard against the Germans in a battle that lasted for a week. Although the German 6th won the fight, the victory was a costly one for Paulus in terms of time, effort, and manpower.

When the two leaders met, Stalin offered Churchill time to explain his position. Churchill emphasized that the British and the Americans were preparing large numbers of troops for a major campaign against the Germans, but he was careful not to mention where or when. He also made it clear that to make even a "small landing in France" would hamper plans to launch a major invasion in 1943.

At first, Stalin paid close attention to Churchill's words. Then, when it became clear the British and Americans were not planning to establish a front in France soon enough to help the Red army, he chastised the prime minister and accused him of being afraid of the Germans. Only then did Churchill reveal to Stalin that an invasion against the Germans in North Africa was planned for later in 1942. This did not make Stalin any happier. He and his people, and the forces of the Red army, needed help immediately.

When the two men met again on August 13, Stalin made it clear to Churchill that he did not support the British leader's plan. He claimed that "the Soviet command built their plan of summer and autumn operations calculating on the creation of a Second Front in Europe in 1942." Stalin was arguing that Churchill and Roosevelt were betraying him. Feeling compelled to offer Stalin something, Churchill promised that the Allies would begin a second front in France in 1943. In reality, the British leader knew that no such front would be established anytime that year.

In the end, little had been gained by the meeting. As historian Walter Kerr explained, "In short, two days of talks at the summit had done nothing to dispel Russian suspicion of the British or British distrust of the Russians." What was clear to Stalin was that his Red army would have to face the continuous onslaught of the German Wehrmacht alone for many more months.

On August 14, the Germans launched a strong attack against the Soviet 4th tank army, pushing those forces back. Tens of thousands of Soviet soldiers were captured by the advancing Germans. Hundreds of Red army tanks were destroyed. Those Soviet troops who made their way back to the relative safety of Stalingrad were plagued by shortages of food and water, a problem made worse by local natives of the steppes, the Kalmucks. These fiercely independent people hated the Communists, and tossed dead animals into wells to make the water undrinkable as Soviet soldiers approached. As the Wehrmacht forces pushed toward the retreating enemy, the German Luftwaffe provided air support. German Stuka dive-bombers destroyed enemy positions, tanks, field headquarters, even civilians.

By August 23, several German tank corps, including the 16th and the 14th Panzer, had completed a spectacular run north of the city and reached the town of Rynok, near the Volga. Stalingrad lay just a few miles to the south. Later in the day, as German infantry troops entered Rynok, they "followed tramcars down the trolley tracks. When passengers looked back and saw troops dressed in strange uniforms, they panicked and jumped off the trains. The Germans laughed. . . ."

Throughout the day, Paulus drove his 6th army to the very outskirts of the city. Panzer divisions drove relentlessly eastward through clouds of hazy dust. Many of the German troops were ecstatic; they knew they were on the verge of their goal, of reaching Stalingrad.

Three separate but coordinated divisions of German troops were zeroing in on Stalingrad by August 23. Paulus was intent on establishing a "forty-mile-long corridor from the Don to the Volga. This barrier of steel would seal off Stalingrad from the north and prevent reinforcements from filtering down to the aid of the city."

By early evening—6:00 P.M.—Paulus's 6th army stood at the edge of the Volga. Surprisingly, many of Stalingrad's people, having been kept in the dark by official reports, had no idea that the troops of the Wehrmacht were ready to invade their city.

Fighting
in the Streets

Once the Germans reached Stalingrad, heated battles took place in the streets and even the buildings of the city. These Soviet soldiers are trying to take over a city block, which would be a major achievement in the fight for Stalingrad.

ven as German tanks rumbled into the city of Stalingrad on the morning of August 24, 1942, loudspeakers at Red Square blared misinformation about possible German air raids. The City Soviet chairman did not want the people to panic. Military reports began to report that there were Germans in the city, "compact columns of trucks and infantry." Thousands of civilians soon received word of the invasion themselves, and throughout the city, they began to take up arms. Political commissars and factory foremen barked instructions to those who were ready to man the defenses. The people were told: "Whoever can bear arms and whoever can shoot, write your names down." Those who did so were handed a rifle and ammunition, along with a white armband to show they were Soviets, since they did not have uniforms.

In the Sunday morning sunlight, 600 German planes neared the city. They approached in V-formations. In the heart of the downtown district, hundreds of Stukas and JU-88s flew in low and began to bomb the red brick buildings. Pandemonium reigned across the city. The long-awaited German assault had finally come with a fury. Historian William Craig described the frenzy of the attack:

> Concussions blew down most of the houses on Gogol and Pushkin streets. Outside a cinema, a woman was decapitated as she ran along the sidewalk. The city waterworks building collapsed from a direct hit. The telephone exchange fell in on itself; all regular phone communications blinked out. The screams of trapped operators came up through a jumble of broken switchboards and control panels. At Stalingrad Pravda ... bombs smashed the outer walls and brought survivors streaming out to seek safety in a nearby cellar. In the meantime, the loudspeakers on Red Square tonelessly asked people to shoulder arms and fight the invader.

By the end of the day, the skies above Stalingrad were heavy with smoke. Much of the city was on fire, burning in the aftermath of repeated attacks by German aircraft. People were running in every direction, uncertain of where they were going or even where they could go. Telephone service was down; electrical lines were down. Explosions punctuated the urban landscape. Whole buildings collapsed as burning timbers split under the weight of mortar and brick. As the sun set, some of the wounded were transported across the river, where they would hopefully be out of harm's way. By dawn the next morning, the Luftwaffe planes again dotted the skies above Stalingrad, continuing their terror from the previous day. The industrial portion

During the continuous bombing by the Germans, the people of Stalingrad searched desperately for places where they would be safe from the fighting. These women and children gathered at the outskirts of the city to escape the danger of the battle.

of town was struck repeatedly. The raids did not end that day or even the next.

At midnight, after nearly 20 hours of massive destruction had been unleashed on his city, the Red army commander who had been assigned to defend Stalingrad telephoned Stalin at the Kremlin. General Andrei Ivanovich Yeremenko informed the Soviet premier that "the situation was very bad, so bad that city officials wanted to blow up some of the factories and transfer the contents of others across the Volga. Stalin would not hear of it. He shouted into the phone at Yeremenko: 'Evacuation and mining of the plants will be interpreted as a decision to surrender Stalingrad.'"

On the streets, political commissars tried to organize

civilian resistance. Posters were plastered around the city. They featured stirring words to rally the dazed victims of Nazi air power:

Dear Comrades!
Native Stalingraders!

Frenzied bands of enemy have reached
walls of our native city.
Bloody Hitlerites are striving to reach sunny Stalingrad
and great Russian river—Volga.
Troops of Red army are selflessly defending Stalingrad.
All approaches to city are strewn with corpses
of German-fascist occupiers.
Super-bandit Hitler is rushing more and more of his cutthroats
into battle and trying to take Stalingrad at any cost.
We will not give up our native city, our native home, our
native land. We will turn every street into impenetrable
barricade. We will make impregnable fortress of
every home, every building, every street.
Soldiers of the Red Army! Defenders of Stalingrad!
We will do everything so you can hold Stalingrad.
Not a step back. Fight enemy without mercy.
Take vengeance on Germans for every hearth destroyed,
for every brutality committed, for bloodshed and tears
of our children, our mothers, and our wives.
Everyone to building barricades!
Everyone who can carry gun—to barricades—
to defense of our native city, our native home.

Thousands responded to these patriotic pleas to defend their homes, and barricades were erected, made from the rubble of buildings that had been standing just days before. At the tractor factory, 3,000 workers united and formed their own military units. Barricade walls spanned the open ground between bombed-out buildings. Repairs were made to buildings and essential systems, such as water. These efforts took place in the midst of chaos caused by the repeated attacks of the Luftwaffe and amid the carnage of death, as bodies littered the streets and bombed-out buildings. In just days, close to 50,000 people had been killed. As German ground forces approached the city, new posters went up. They called on each male in the city between the ages of 18 and 50 to take up arms. Tens of thousands "enlisted" and were sent to the urban front with no uniform and only a few days of training at most. Some went to the fight dressed in their nicest Sunday clothes.

As the Germans moved on Stalingrad, they came from the north, through the suburbs. This move managed to separate several Red army units. The Wehrmacht troops also cut off Soviet communication lines. Still, the men of the German 6th army did not enter the city in a hurry. By the early morning hours of August 24, the 16th Panzer, positioned on the edge of Stalingrad, was far ahead of its supply line. The vehicles of the 60th motorized division had become bottlenecked. The Germans were forced to maneuver large numbers of troops, as well as tanks and other motorized vehicles over a limited amount of terrain. As it pressed toward the city, the Wehrmacht was losing mobility—the one factor that had always been a key part of their blitzkrieg tactics. "Lightning warfare" was out of the question now.

Many of the German leaders pressing in on Stalingrad understood that it was vital to bring down the city in a short period of time. To fail to do so would mean the Germans would have to fight a campaign that dragged into September and October, and then the snows would fall again. They would be forced to spend the winter there, just as they had done the previous winter at the gates of Leningrad and Moscow. The Germans also faced the usual worry: Only so many German troops were on hand to bring about the fall of

Stalingrad. The Soviets, however, could devote nearly limitless numbers of troops to the same battle. Facing the might of the German 6th army, the Russians were able to bring in large numbers of troops. Before the end of August, the Soviet 8th and 9th reserve armies had been activated for duty in Stalingrad, along with two newly formed tank corps, as well as five rifle divisions. These forces alone represented nearly 200,000 "fresh" troops the Red army could bring to the fighting at Stalingrad. The Germans had no such reserves. In the days, weeks, and months ahead, the Germans, including Hitler himself, would come to realize that it had been much easier to *reach* the city of Stalingrad than it would be to bring about the city's collapse.

A Russian Fighter Named Tania

Among the ranks fighting desperately to defend the city of Stalingrad were several hearty women, who took part in the fighting with a measure of skill, tenacity, and courage equal to that of any of the men. One of these women was a 20-year-old blonde named Tania Chernova.

Chernova arrived in Stalingrad on September 23, as part of the 284th division. Although she had not grown up expecting to be a soldier (one of her early dreams was to become a ballerina) when the Germans invaded her homeland, she knew she had to fight. Her first experiences in the field were as a partisan fighter in the dark woods of Belorussia and the Ukraine. On the day she rode a barge across the Volga River to join at the fighting in Stalingrad, a German bomber struck the transport vessel, killing several of her comrades and throwing Chernova into the water. After swimming to shore, she and several others hid in a sewer tunnel. Chernova made her way through the confusion of enemy lines (at one point, Tania sat down at a soldier's dinner table, only to realize it was a German camp), then joined a group of street fighters.

Chernova became a spirited defender of Stalingrad. She trained with enthusiasm and lived alongside her comrades, almost all of whom were men. She found herself "living in foxholes, drinking vodka, eating with a spoon she kept

By August 25, the 16th Panzer assaulted Red army positions north of Stalingrad, attempting to break through the defenses surrounding the city. The assault met with a "withering fire from hastily fortified Soviet trenches." Armed with machine guns and mortars, the Russians fought tenaciously in the face of enemy tanks. At one point, the Russians actually mounted a small counterattack, using T-34 tanks that had been driven straight from the factory floor and were still unpainted. When the commander of the 16th Panzer, General Hans Hube, called for additional support, he discovered that other German forces were also under heavy fire. The Russian 35th guards division was desperately fighting the Wehrmacht 3rd motorized division,

in her boot." In time, Chernova became one of Vassili Zaitsev's sniper students, learning the skills of tracking targets, whom she referred to as "sticks" to keep herself from thinking of them as human beings.

The young Russian faced danger every day. On one mission, she and five men were ordered to blow up a German outpost located near the Red October Factory. At night, the six fighters crawled across the rubble of Stalingrad until they reached the building. As she climbed stealthily up a staircase, a German soldier surprised Chernova, holding a gun to her face. Refusing to surrender, she kicked the soldier in the groin and fought him off until one of her comrades rushed down the stairs and bashed the German in the head with a rifle. The Russian group returned to their task, set the dynamite charge, and rushed from the building, drawing enemy fire. They took satisfaction in the success of their mission when they heard a violent explosion behind them.

During the three months that Chernova served in Stalingrad before she was severely wounded in a mine explosion, she was credited with killing 80 German soldiers. For decades after the war, she continued to refer to the enemy combatants she struck down as "sticks" that she had "broken."

forcing the Germans into a circular defensive formation called a "hedgehog." With thousands of men backed by Red army tanks, the Russian 35th was accomplishing exactly what it needed to: It was dividing the parts of the 14th Panzer from one another. When General Paulus received radio dispatches from his separated divisions, he knew he "faced the chilling prospect of losing one or more of these units unless he could send enough reinforcements and supplies to help them forge that barrier of steel to the Volga."

Though Paulus's units met strong resistance at the north end of the city, the Luftwaffe planes had already managed to destroy much of the infrastructure and buildings of Stalingrad. Red Square and almost 100 downtown blocks were in ruin, having been leveled by air attack. Fires were burning everywhere. Nearly all the city waterworks were inoperable, so it was impossible to fight the fires. In the industrial sector, workers at the tractor factory had taken up positions throughout the huge complex. They watched as Red army troops and armed civilians stormed past the factory toward the Mokraya Mechetka River to reinforce their comrades, who faced well-trained German combat troops.

Since the attack on the city began, barges filled with civilian refugees had been making repeated crossings to the east bank of the Volga. The crossing was extremely dangerous. German planes dove in close, sometimes just 100 feet (31 meters) above the water, strafing the boats with machine-gun fire. Along the west bank of the Volga, Stukas bombed the frightened civilians. Historian William Craig described the scene:

> With no place to hide, the masses there weaved back and forth like a pendulum, first close to the cliff wall for shelter and then out again when the Stukas dove past. Clusters of bombs found them and the shoreline was slippery with blood. Medical teams pulled the dead from

the footpaths as the living pushed each other on to the boats that were to evacuate them. . . . In the hazy sunlight of the warm afternoon, the Volga erupted in a chain of fierce explosions, and several boats of the rescue fleet broke apart and sank with almost no survivors. The surface of the river was soon dotted with bodies, bobbing lazily in the current.

For days, the German assaults on the ground were met by spirited Soviet defenses. Yeremenko's forces fought valiantly to maintain any ground they gained. More was needed, however. The Germans had come 1,500 miles (2,414 kilometers) from their homeland, and they were not about to abandon their campaign. To make matters worse, Russian morale was running low. German field reports from Paulus's 6th army told of many Russians surrendering and crossing over to German lines: "Many deserters, some even coming in . . . with their tanks."

One Russian colonel, dealing with low spirits among his forces, which were part of the Soviet 64th division, situated 25 miles (40 kilometers) north of Stalingrad, found a unique way to counter the flagging resolve of his men, who had been deserting in increasing numbers. He called a general assembly of his regiments, and as they stood in lines at attention, he berated them harshly, accusing them of treason and dereliction of duty. He said they were cowards, telling them it was their responsibility that their comrades had deserted. Demanding that they stand and fight for Russia, the colonel reinforced his point by pulling out his gun. As he marched down a line of soldiers, he counted off until he reached the tenth man. Then he turned and shot that soldier in the head. He repeated this same action down the line, killing every tenth man, until he had emptied his pistol and six Russians lay dead.

By August 27, Stalin, from his headquarters in Moscow's

Kremlin, sent a new commander to Stalingrad. He appointed Marshal Georgi Konstantinovich Zhukov, who had led Soviet forces in the Leningrad siege of the previous year. Having fought through two sieges already, Zhukov, now bearing a newly created title, deputy supreme commander of the Red army, was the best leader the Soviet army had to help the troops face down the Germans at Stalingrad.

By August 28, after five days of bitter fighting, the Germans began to experience some breaks in their efforts against the Red army. That day, a German train was able to deliver 500 freight cars of food and ammunition to General Hube's 16th Panzer division, which was on the verge of being overrun. Although the 16th had failed to defeat the Soviet defenders at the tractor factory, with new supplies, Hube could now refocus his efforts. At the same time, the 3rd motorized division had reunited with the 16th Panzer, blocking off a 16-mile-long (26-kilometer-long) stretch of territory between Stalingrad and the Don River. The 60th motorized was also matching Soviet thrusts blow for blow.

As Paulus retooled his strategy, he began to order the main body of his forces from Kalatsch directly east—straight toward Stalingrad. Only the last remains of the Soviet 62nd army, which numbered 25,000 men at best, stood in the path of Paulus's new invasion. In a coordinated effort, General Hermann Hoth's 4th Panzers began to move his tanks to the west in an effort to slip around Russian defenses. If successful, Hoth's and Paulus's two advances could create a pincer and squeeze out the Russians in their paths.

By the evening of August 29, this threat caused Yeremenko to pull his men back from their positions south and southwest of Stalingrad. The move was a serious gamble. Although it might save large numbers of Soviet troops for the moment, it could also leave Stalingrad very vulnerable. The Germans detected the movements of the retreating Russians and thousands of Soviets were captured on August 30 as "trucks, tanks, and hundreds of artillery pieces dropped into German hands without a fight."

Hoth was delighted. The western door to the city on the Volga appeared to have opened as if by magic. He dispatched his Panzers to reconnoiter with Paulus' forces. Then, however, surprisingly, Paulus did not sent his tanks toward Hoth's to make a joint assault on the city. Having faced days of repeated, desperate Russian attacks, Paulus was not prepared to risk his forces on an unlikely gamble. By failing to move, Paulus lost his opportunity to capture 20,000 trapped Red army forces, which had time to escape under orders from Yeremenko. When Paulus finally did move, on September 2, it was too late. Those three days of delay would prove to be extremely important. Rather than defeat the Russians out in the rural steppe country, the fight would now center on the rubble-strewn streets of Stalingrad.

The man Stalin had appointed to be the savior of Stalingrad, General Zhukov, had arrived in the city by August 29. Zhukov found the forces defending the urban center and its outlying suburbs ready and willing to fight, but woefully short of ammunition. He also noticed a severe lack of coordination among the infantry, tank divisions, and air units. His calls to Stalin in Moscow brought no orders as to how to fix these problems. The Soviet premier simply told Zhukov to defeat the enemy by September 5. When Zhukov tried to press Stalin for help, the Soviet leader hung up the phone.

Whereas Stalin was undoubtedly disappointed by the lack of Soviet success against the Germans, Adolf Hitler was equally frustrated. As the German Group A's 1st Panzer and 17th armies continued their march south toward the Caucasus and its oil fields, they met with stiff resistance and a Russian scorched-earth policy. Avoiding a direct field battle, the Russians lured the Germans farther and farther away from their supply lines, while they destroyed their own oil centers before the Wehrmacht forces could reach them. By the end of August, German Field Marshal Sigmund Wilhelm List could see no reason to continue his advance. When he suggested this to Hitler, however, the German leader "went into a tirade and threatened to fire him." Even so, by the early fall of 1942, one thing was becoming painfully clear to the Germans, including Adolf Hitler: "Germans had the brains and the ability and the mobility to inflict casualties and gain ground, [but] they did not have the strength to take Stalingrad and the Caucasus at the same time."

Far from the battlefields of Russia, Hitler could only do so much to change the direction and course of events taking place daily in the heat of August and early September. From his headquarters in the Ukraine, Hitler made himself the commander of Group A. The move would bring disastrous results.

Back on the Stalingrad front, the conflict between the Germans and Russians seemed to be on the verge of a dramatic shift. Through the first days of September, three Soviet armies whose ranks were filled with new, untrained recruits, were dispatched to the front north of the city. Although the Soviets had no battle experience and held inadequate artillery, the 6th German army was slightly weakened itself.

At the same time—on September 12—General Yeremenko appointed a new commander to the demoralized Russian 62nd army. He was General Vassili Chuikov, and he would prove to be the right man for the difficult job of boosting the morale of the 62nd and bringing about a turning point in the conflict. Chuikov, the son of a peasant, had worked as a bellhop before the Russian Revolution. He took part in the civil war that had brought the Communist party to power. He was a loyal Red army commander, one who never questioned his orders, especially if they were issued directly by Stalin. The stocky black-haired military leader was a no-nonsense man. He paid so little attention to his personal appearance that he was "frequently mistaken for the average foot soldier."

When Chuikov took command of the 62nd, the unit was on its last legs. It had faced hard fighting against the Germans on the west banks of the Don River in earlier weeks, and was extremely war-weary. Pushed back to Stalingrad, the 62nd had been forced to set up a front-line defense around the Dzerhezinsky Tractor Factory, where it faced the brunt of the German assault on the city from the north. The unit's numbers had dwindled dramatically through weeks of fighting. The story of its losses lies in the numbers: "An armored brigade possessed just one tank. An infantry brigade counted exactly 666 soldiers, of whom only 200 were qualified riflemen. A regiment which should have mustered 3000 troops listed 100. The division next to it, normally 10,000 strong, had a total of 1500." When Chuikov took command on the night of September 12, the 62nd army was a fighting force of only 50,000 men.

Chuikov was a realist. In taking command of the 62nd, an army of limited numbers and resources, he knew a change in tactic was needed. He organized the 62nd into units called "storm groups," that he believed could be used to counterweigh the German advantages in troop numbers, air support, and artillery. Dozens of squads, each numbering between 10 and 20 men, were assigned positions in various buildings around the city. Each stationed squad would become a minitarget for advancing German troops. The enemy would have limited access, though. Planes would serve no purpose, since, in such tight circumstances, the Luftwaffe Stukas could not bomb targets without the risk of killing their own troops. As tanks rolled through the city, drawn by the presence of small groups of urban defenders, the Soviet soldiers could ambush them, using artillery guns placed in strategic sites. The crux of Chuikov's plan was to put the German troops at a disadvantage by forcing them to fight in the streets, where they would often be sitting ducks at the hands of well-hidden, increasingly skilled urban guerrilla fighters. The success of the Russian struggle for Stalingrad, said Chuikov, "did not depend on strength, but on ability, skill, daring, guile. Buildings split up enemy formations like breakwaters, forcing them to follow the line of the streets. . . . These buildings allowed us to set up centers of resistance from which the defenders mowed down the Nazis with their automatic weapons."

House-to-house fights raged across the city. The Germans might occupy the first floor of a building, while Soviet street fighters controlled the second and third floors. There were always fires burning, and a pall of smoke seemed to hang in the air for days. Movement was chaotic. There was no front line. Battles were fought for control of a neighborhood, a block, a building, even a room. According to historian Walter Kerr, "There were times when the Russians held a kitchen, the Germans, the living room." In a Stalingrad print shop, Russian fighters managed to fight their way to the building's first floor, only to have the Germans take over the upper floor. When the Russian street guerrillas finally took control of the second floor, the Germans had found a way downstairs, occupying the ground floor once again.

Much of the street fighting in Stalingrad was tenuous. Captured buildings did not always remain in the same hands, even for a short period of time. Excerpts from a Soviet military diary from September 14 express some of the frustration of this indecisive urban fighting:

0730:   [7:30 A.M.] the enemy has reached Academy Street.
0740:   1st Battalion 38th Mechanized Brigade is cut off from our main forces.
0750:   fighting has flared up in the sector of Mamaev-Kurgan hill and in the streets leading to the station.
0800:   the station is in enemy hands.
0840:   the station is in our hands.
0940:   the station has been retaken by the enemy

During the lengthy battle for Stalingrad, houses within the city became strategic points in the advance of each army. Fierce fighting might occur for control of a particular house, or even one floor or room of a house.

Sometimes the street action was put on hold as combatants played a waiting game, intent on discovering a weakness in the enemy before striking. The following scene was probably played out in thousands of variations during the siege of Stalingrad: A ten-man German squad dashes across the industrial district near the tractor factory. They find shelter inside the front room of a bombed-out industrial shop. Only then do the Germans realize that some Russian fighters are hiding on the second floor. One of the Germans takes a pack of explosives, called a "satchel charge," and tosses it up the staircase toward the hiding Russians. With quick movement, a Russian soldier grabs the pack and tosses it back down the stairs. The explosion wounds several Germans instead of the original Russian targets.

Uncertain how to approach the Russians on the second

floor, the Germans wait overnight, sleeping two men at a time, while the others keep watch at every door, window, and, of course, the staircase. There is no sound from upstairs throughout the night. The next morning, two Russians, armed with machine guns, slip down the stairs, unleash a hail of bullets, then bound back upstairs. The Germans consider scaling a freight elevator to reach the second floor, but reject the idea because it would be too noisy. The German squad leader finally reaches someone on his walkie-talkie and explains where he and his men are—"We are in the third white house"—and then the squad waits the rest of the day until reinforcements get into their position outside the occupied house.

German sharpshooters set up in neighboring buildings, trying to sight their targets. After several single rifle shots, the Germans creep up the stairs, nervous and tense. They reach the door at the top of the steps, count silently, then break the door in with a sudden crash. They find evidence that the deadly work of the German sharpshooters was successful. Seven Russian bodies lie scattered across the floor. The Germans are finally able to take over the house.

In addition to scenes like that, some of the street fighting involved trained Russian snipers. At the Lazur Chemical Plant, which covered a city block, the Russians set up a school for sharpshooters. Along a lengthy stretch of factory wall were painted outlines of human bodies, helmets, and observation slits, which served as targets for would-be Russian gunmen who needed to practice. Anyone who showed promise with a rifle was sent into the city, where he could move quietly, firing at the enemy, one soldier at a time. Sometimes these deadly assassins moved in pairs or larger groups to provide cover for one another.

One such Russian sniper was destined to become famous among both his own people and the Germans. Vassili Zaitsev arrived in Stalingrad as part of the 284th division, a young man from the Ural Mountains, where he had grown up tending sheep. When he came to the city on the Volga, he was already skilled with a rifle. It was a talent he had gained hunting deer back home. Referring to him by name, Russian newspapers told his story, and he became a terrifying figure to the Germans. In just ten days, according to Communist propaganda, Zaitsev had killed 40 Germans, each with a single rifle shot. In time, the legendary Russian sharpshooter was assigned to train dozens of additional Russian snipers.

As Zaitsev's reputation grew, the Germans decided that he was one Russian they had to eliminate. A German major named Konings was brought in from Berlin. His sole purpose was to stalk and kill Zaitsev. When he arrived, he studied the bombed-out city, reviewed Russian materials describing sniper training methods, and learned about Zaitsev and his own habits as a sniper. The Russians heard about Konings and his mission from a captured prisoner. Zaitsev was informed, and a curious and tense duel soon began.

When two Russian snipers were killed by single rifle shots, Zaitsev believed that Konings had to be the assassin. Zaitsev moved to the desolate stretch of landscape between the Red October plant and Mamaev Hill and searched with binoculars for his would-be killer. For several days, Zaitsev and a fellow sniper looked for the German sniper without success. Konings was there, but he was a professional. He would not reveal himself before he had discovered Zaitsev's position.

On the third day, Zaitsev and his fellow sniper, Nikolai Kulikov, were accompanied by a political writer named Danilov who was intent on reporting the strange two-man contest. To lure Konings out, Danilov exposed his position, stood up, and shouted: "There he is. I'll point him out to you." Instinctively, Konings fired at Danilov, wounding him. His response, however, gave Zaitsev enough information to determine where the wily German major was hiding. To make certain, Zaitsev placed a glove on a stick and raised it up. A rifle cracked, and a bullet whizzed through the exposed glove. Now, Zaitsev knew for certain where Konings was situated.

Silently, the two Russian sharpshooters crept from their positions until they had the sun at their backs, leaving Konings to fire into the streaming afternoon light. They waited until the next day to engage the German. That afternoon, with the sun blinding Konings's vision, the Russians sited their rifle scopes on their unsuspecting target. Suddenly, the glass from the German's scope reflected in the sun. Kulikov raised a helmet on a stick, Konings fired, and the Russian stood, pretending to be shot. Only when the German sniper lowered his rifle to get a better look at his latest kill did the still-hidden Zaitsev fire a single shot, sending a lethal bullet between Konings's eyes.

Although the story of the duel between Zaitsev and Konings has the makings of a genuine, personalized thriller in the midst of a wide-ranging larger battle, some historians are skeptical about the facts. Some doubt the tale altogether. In his 1998 book, *Stalingrad: The Fateful Siege*, Stalingrad scholar Antony Beevor wrote of the alleged duel:

> Some Soviet sources claim that the Germans brought in the chief of their sniper school to hunt down Zaitsev, but that Zaitsev outwitted him. . . . The telescopic sight of his prey's rifle, allegedly Zaitsev's most treasured trophy, is still exhibited in the Moscow armed forces museum, but this dramatic story remains essentially unconvincing. . . . It is worth noting that there is absolutely no mention of [the duel] in any of the reports to [Chief of the Red Army political department], Shcherbakov, even though almost every aspect of "sniperism" was reported with relish.

Whatever lingering doubts may exist concerning this most famous of Zaitsev's kills, the sniper from the Urals remained a part of the fighting at Stalingrad through the entire siege. In the final weeks of the urban fight, he was severely wounded, temporarily blinded as a result of an explosion near the Red October plant. He survived his wounds and ended his days as a sharpshooter with 242 German kills to his credit.

Still, the battle for the heart and soul of Stalingrad dragged on. Street fighting raged in every corner and square of the bombed-out buildings until no one—Russian civilian, Soviet fighter, or German soldier—could cross from one building to another without expecting to be shot at. A German lieutenant described the situation:

> The Street is no longer measured by meters but by corpses ... We have fought for fifteen days for a single house with mortars, grenades, machine-guns and bayonets. Already by the third day fifty-four German corpses are strewn in the cellars, on the landings, and the staircases. The front is a corridor between burnt-out rooms; it is the thin ceiling between two floors. Help comes from neighboring houses by fire-escapes and chimneys. There is a ceaseless struggle from noon to night. From story to story, faces black with sweat, we bombed each other with grenades in the middle of explosions, clouds of dust and smoke. . . . Ask any soldier what hand-to-hand struggle means in such a fight. ... Stalingrad is no longer a town. By day it is an enormous cloud of burning, blinding smoke; it is a vast furnace lit by the reflection of the flames.

Turning the
Tide of Battle

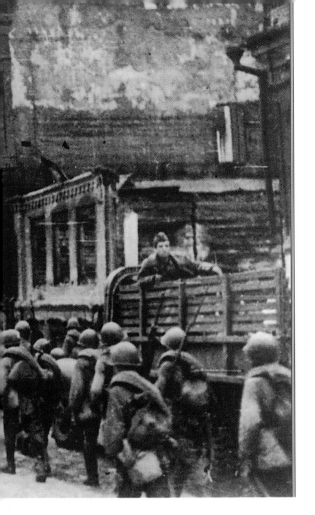

The Soviets' biggest advantage over the Germans was their ability to find reinforcements whenever necessary. In January 1943, additional Soviet troops arrived in Stalingrad to help take the city back from the German army.

As the war dragged on, the German forces increasingly suffered the effects of attrition. Dead German soldiers could not be replaced. Ruined equipment, tanks, and artillery were simply considered gone. The Russians, on the other hand, were able to resupply their forces—in everything from guns to manpower— through the entire battle for the city. In the early weeks of the urban struggle, the Soviets were hampered by "the incompetent meddling of political commissars in military operations," which typically led to "gross errors and created difficulties for the military commanders." By early October 1942, however, the commissars were removed and command of the Stalingrad action became more coherent and cooperative.

The system became well oiled, less hampered by paperwork and politics, and the Red army fighters and their civilian counter-parts were well supplied. Industrial production from factories and plants far to the east, out of harm's way, produced large quantities of supplies and equipment. From July through the end of 1942, Soviet factories built 15,800 fighter planes (fully 60 percent more than were built in the first half of the year), plus 13,600 tanks and nearly 16,000 artillery pieces. By November, the Soviets had 40 percent more tanks and motor-ized artillery and 30 percent more field guns and mortars than the Germans had. They also had 10 percent more planes than the Luftwaffe commanded in the Stalingrad region.

As the fighting raged in the city, the Red army sent increasing numbers of troops to Stalingrad. This fact alone was perhaps the most demoralizing factor for the Germans. Each Wehrmacht soldier knew that, despite any gains made in street fighting during the day, "every night hundreds of ferries brought in reinforcements across the Volga and there was no way of stopping them."

On September 13, the day after Chuikov had arrived to take command of the Soviet 62nd, the Germans launched a series of massive attacks on the city, in an attempt to destroy all Red army resistance. The attack included the German 29th motorized division, the 295th, 71st, and 94th infantry divisions, and the 14th and 24th Panzer divisions. The coor-dinated assaults made significant headway within hours, including the capture of the Soviet 62nd army headquarters. The city railway station was captured on September 14, after it had changed hands several times between German forces and Russian street fighters.

Reinforcements were ferried across the Volga to give the besieged Red army some relief. On the night of September 15, the 13th guards division and two additional infantry divisions, plus an infantry brigade and an armored brigade, landed on the west docks of Stalingrad. When the 13th division arrived, the men "ran a gauntlet of machine gun and artillery fire to establish a bridgehead from which they made a succession of sharp counter-attacks." The Red army 13th managed to halt the German advance. Its casualties were extremely high, though. By mid-October, this army, which had numbered 10,000 when they arrived in Stalingrad in mid-September, had been reduced to just a few hundred men.

Soviet commanders continued to meet the German assaults with more and more troops. On September 17, the Soviet 92nd rifle brigade arrived, along with the 137th tank brigade. Despite some short-lived field successes, however, the Soviets were losing the battle. Even significant counter-attacks failed to break the German advance. Paulus and his 6th army appeared to be succeeding, much to Hitler's delight.

For the moment, Paulus's victories continued. With Luftwaffe support, units of the German 6th army reached the banks of the Volga by September 20, downstream from the railway station they had captured earlier in the week. This movement placed Chuikov's forces in a jam. The 62nd army was separated from the 64th army, where its troops were caught with the river to their backs.

For six weeks, the battle for the streets and the destiny of Stalingrad raged. General Chuikov, commander of the Soviet 62nd army, described the fighting as a continuous boxing match: "It was like a boxer who has been called on to go from one ring to another without a break and fight opponents of varying weights; before the last fight there had not even been time enough to take a deep breath and wipe the sweat away." Even as the fight for the city became the central focus of Soviet forces in the region, however, other strategies were being put into effect, designed not only to remove the Wehrmacht from the streets of the city on the Volga, but to drive them off Soviet soil completely.

Just before the start of the German attacks on September 13, Russian commanders had already formulated a plan "for a full-scale counter-offensive, aimed at encircling the German

Together, Soviet Marshals Konstantin Rokossovsky (left) and Georgi Zhukov (right) planned the Russian counterattack that took place in the fall of 1942. This photograph was taken later, in 1945, when these two famous leaders met with British Field Marshal Montgomery (center) in Berlin.

6th Army. The fate of Paulus' army was being plotted before it had even begun its assault on Stalingrad." Marshal Konstantin Rokossovsky and Marshal Georgi Konstantinovich Zhukov were the chief architects of the plan to launch a massive Soviet counteroffensive that fall. The plan was approved by Stalin and officially named "Operation Uranus" on September 28. It was then that Zhukov suggested that Rokossovsky take command of the Stalingrad front.

Between them, Zhukov and Rokossovsky had always understood one clear fact about the Battle of Stalingrad: "[The] battle for the city would soak up battalions, regiments, whole divisions—and that the main body of the 6th Army would be sucked into the maelstrom, leaving its long flanks guarded by second-rate units." Confident that the number of Soviet forces would always include a strong reserve of troops, Zhukov and Rokossovsky intended to "not just cut off the Germans in Stalingrad, but to push all the way to the Black Sea coast and amputate Army Group A. A third . . . [blow] would fall simultaneously on Army Group Center." "The plan of the Soviet command was to use the forces of three fronts, the Southwestern, the Stalingrad, and the Don, to encircle the German armies between the Volga and the Don, and then destroy them." The intended result was to remove the threat of all German forces in the Stalingrad region, including the Caucasus, and destroy Hitler's dreams of bringing the Soviet Union to its knees.

Already, the German forces in the Caucasus were running into trouble. Group A had driven relentlessly to the oil fields near Grozny and to the edge of the city of Astrakhan on the Volga Delta near the Caspian Sea. Such field success had placed the German units 600 miles (966 kilometers) from Stalingrad and beyond the extent of their supply lines, however. By November 1, the 13th Panzer division arrived outside Ordzhonikidze, south of Grozny, in the heart of the Caucasus Mountains. Here, the Soviets launched an effective counterattack that forced Hitler's tanks to turn around or face defeat. Two weeks later, the North Caucasus and the Trans-Caucasus fronts—representing a total of 22 Axis divisions (including six Romanian and one Slovak) were facing 90 "major formations, including 37 infantry and eight or nine cavalry divisions, and eight armored brigades. The tide was about to turn on Germany's effort to secure Caucasian oil."

October, then, became the month during which the Battle of Stalingrad turned toward Soviet victory over the Wehrmacht forces of Hitler. It was a long month, though. The German offensive continued relentlessly, as General Paulus sent his 6th army forces against the Dzerhezinsky

Tractor Factory and the Barrikady Gun Factory complex on October 14. The next two weeks witnessed yet another act in the deadly drama that had engulfed Stalingrad for months:

> On 14 October the Germans struck out; that day will go down as the bloodiest and most ferocious of the whole battle. Along a narrow front of four or five kilometers, the Germans threw in five infantry divisions and two tank divisions supported by masses of artillery and planes . . . during the day there were over two thousand Luftwaffe sorties. That morning you could not hear the separate shots or explosions, the whole merged into one continuous deafening roar. At five yards you could no longer distinguish anything, so thick were the dust and smoke. . . . That day sixty-one men in my headquarters were killed.

Over the next four days, the two armies fought for control of the city. By October 18, in some parts of Stalingrad, the Russian front had been pushed back to within 300 yards (274 meters) of the Volga. Germans were in the vicinity of the Red October Factory. The tractor plant was also close to falling into enemy hands. Men fought without mercy, giving thought only to the strategic value of bombed-out buildings. As one historian later wrote: "For every house, workshop, water-tower, railway embankment, wall, cellar and every pile of ruins a bitter battle was waged, without equal even in the First World War." Their nerves racked, the fighting men of the German 6th army and the Red army's 62nd infantry were locked in a human struggle of extraordinary proportions:

> [The] fighting raged day and night, [with] German combat engineer teams spearheading each assault with flame throwers and explosive charges. Tanks surrounded by infantry protection teams fired into Soviet strong

points at point blank range, and Stukas appeared over Stalingrad every morning, bombing with great precision. By November only ten percent of the city remained in Russian hands, the ruins of the tractor factory were finally captured and Chuikov's army was split in two.

Then, on November 11, the 6th army launched attacks against the Red October steelworks, blitzing the grounds with nine concentrated divisions. Even as it made the assault, elements of the 6th were completely worn out, battle-weary, and drastically reduced in numbers. Entire companies of riflemen could claim only two to three dozen men. Of the thousands of tanks the 6th had rolled across the steppes of Russia, only 180 were still in operation.

Meanwhile, during that same week, Russian forces were massing outside the city, to the north, along a 200-mile (322-kilometer) front then held by forces of the Axis powers, including Hungarian, Italian, and Romanian divisions. The Soviet command, intent on carrying out a counteroffensive on a truly massive scale, provided as much support in terms of troops and materiel as possible. Half of the Red army's available reserve of artillery was moved into the Stalingrad region for the counteroffensive. This reserve included a total of 230 artillery regiments, troops who had at their disposal 13,540 cannons and mortar. Four Soviet air forces were also dispatched: two to the southwest front and one each for the Stalingrad and Don fronts, bringing the total air support for the coming campaign to 1,000 planes, including 600 fighters.

The Soviet Command understood that the success of their planned counteroffensive would depend on surprising the Germans. To that end, secrecy about every facet of the plan was strictly maintained. Troop movements, as well as the delivery of equipment, was done under cover of darkness. Russian radio operators misled German listening-posts by sending messages as if the units they were assigned to were still operating in the same vicinity when, in reality, they had already moved to a different location. Apparently, the Soviet deceit worked. One high-ranking German officer, writing in 1943, stated: "We had no idea of the gigantic concentrations of Russian forces on the flank of the 6th Army. Shortly before the attacks, there was nothing there and suddenly we were struck a massive blow." Even as Field Marshal Paulus "deduced that the enemy was preparing some pincer movement," which caused him to order the 14th Panzer division across the Don River to support his left flank, "he could do no more as he had the strictest orders from Hitler to hold Stalingrad at all costs."

Thus, with more than one million troops massed, backed with nearly 1,000 tanks and an equal number of planes, as well as nearly 14,000 pieces of artillery and mortar, the daring Soviets launched their counteroffensive at 7:30 A.M. on November 19. The Germans were hit hard by two violent movements. The first was a well-coordinated series of attacks that included "the thunderous roar of a hundred multiple-rocket launcher batteries," and hundreds of Red army planes dotting the skies above hundreds of miles of German-held territory. The second was a harsh winter snowstorm that engulfed the city of Stalingrad, as the Russian winter set in and helped the battered combatants of the Soviet Union.

The massive Soviet assault was concentrated along three separately operating fronts: the southwest, the Don, and the Stalingrad. Success came immediately for the Red army. As Luftwaffe planes were grounded by the Arctic weather, the Russians swarmed against units of the Romanian and Italian armies south of the Don River. Soviet field artillery, numbering about 90 per mile, cut the enemy deep and quickly. The artillery barrage destroyed the Romanian 3rd army's telephone lines, which cut the Axis troops off from their German commanders. After just over an hour of heavy shelling, Russian commanders ordered tanks and infantry to move against the unprepared enemy. A heavy fog provided good cover, masking the Red army's movements until it was too late for the Romanians to respond adequately.

Along the southwest front, the Soviet 5th tank army met with stiff resistance from some Romanian units. Even so, before the day was over, that resistance flagged. By nightfall, Soviet tanks had Romanian forces retreating in a panic. Meanwhile, to the east, the Soviet 21st army pushed ahead along a 9-mile-long (14.5-kilometer-long) front and managed to repeat the success of the 5th tank army. By sunset on November 19, the Romanian V armored corps was almost completely surrounded.

Elsewhere, the Russians did not have such dramatic field success against German forces. Along the Don front, the Soviet 65th army fought the German XI Corps, which made up the bulk of Paulus's left flank. Rugged terrain impeded the movement of Russian tanks and the 14th Panzer division was able to launch a counterattack. The day ended with limited gains for the Red army.

As the battle began that morning, several German units responded quickly and were sent into the fight expecting to stop the unsuspected Soviet attack. The 48th Panzer was in the battle by 9:30 A.M. with orders to assault what was believed to be the main line of the Russian offensive, near Kletskaya, northwest of Stalingrad. Less than two hours later, however, amid great confusion, the 48th was ordered to change direction entirely. Hampered by the fog, the 48th lost contact with its support units, including the 22nd Panzer and the Romanian 1st armored division, both of which accidentally ran into the Soviet 5th tank army. By day's end, those two Axis units had been delivered into the hands of the Soviets.

Along the Stalingrad front, the Russians placed their hopes on three units—the 51st, 57th, and 64th armies. Together, they met opposition from Field Marshal Hoth's 4th Panzer corps and the 4th Romanian army. Although the

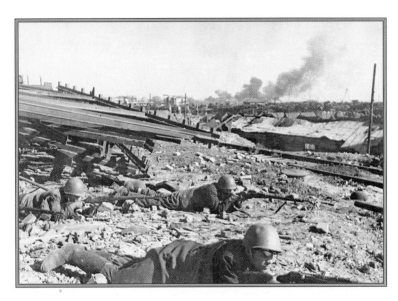

The Soviet counteroffensive took place in November 1943. These members of a worker's battalion defended their plant from the Nazis on the outskirts of Stalingrad. Although the Russians suffered heavy losses, they were eventually able to surround the German forces on the perimeter of the city.

heavy fog postponed the attack until 1:00 P.M., when Red army forces moved forward, they crushed the Romanian 6th corps, almost completely destroying three divisions. Within 24 hours, any significant Axis opposition to the three Russian armies was gone.

Each of the Russian victories of November 19–20 helped create a strong line of Red army strength that was slowly surrounding the Germans and their fellow Axis armies. By November 22, just three days after the Russian counteroffensive began, some Red army units had advanced as far forward as 60 miles (97 kilometers). The attack had clearly caught the Axis forces off-guard. On the morning of November 20, the Soviet 5th tank army, with support from the 4th tank corps and the 3rd guards corps, surprised the Romanian II corps completely. In fact, once the Soviets overran the Romanian positions, they entered the enemy's headquarters, where they "found tables laden with maps and documents, cupboards open, keys in the locks of chests, teleprinters still connected, and officers' caps still hanging on their pegs."

The Russians were able to capture the main bridge spanning the Don River through a bit of clever trickery. Russian forces manned five captured German tanks and drove them toward the bridge with their lights on, as the Germans typically drove them. Each tank carried 12 Soviet soldiers armed with sub-machine guns. As they approached the German bridge-guard, the Soviets surprised the German guards and occupied the bridge. Over November 23–24, the Russians made more gains. Parts of Stalingrad front forces met units from the Don front south of the town of Kalatsch, west of Stalingrad.

Throughout those opening days of the offensive, the Soviets had feared that the German and Axis units would avoid being surrounded or captured by breaking out to safety, away from Stalingrad. This was unlikely, however, since all appeals German leaders made to Hitler during the offensive to allow units to abandon their positions were refused by the German dictator. He simply would not allow his troops to give up any territory under their control. "I won't go back from the Volga," Hitler had sternly informed Paulus. The decision left Hitler's forces to fight for ground they could not continue to hold.

Within just days, a formerly defensive force had turned the war over Stalingrad into another sort of siege. By November 23, the Russians had successfully encircled more than 300,000 German forces, including the entire 6th army, within the confines of Stalingrad itself. It was a stunning victory, and the timing could not have been worse for the Germans. Already, a merciless Russian winter was howling at the Wehrmacht's door.

No Way Out

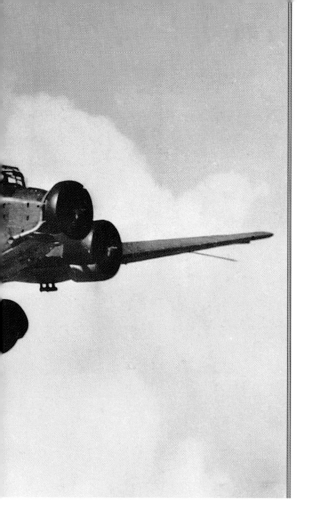

The Germans caused some of the greatest destruction with their powerful air force, the Luftwaffe. Junkers 52 were used by the German air force for military transport throughout the war.

In its short and successful counteroffensive, the Red army had captured a considerable number of German units and their equipment. Any possible escape for the Germans would come at a high cost, including the abandonment of Hitler's dream of conquering the Soviet Union.

Hitler did not appear to panic in the face of the turnabout in Stalingrad after the Soviet counteroffensive. He did not believe, or at least would not publicly admit, that the setback was permanent. He referred to Paulus's situation as "a temporary encirclement." Intent on keeping Paulus in Stalingrad, Hitler promised to supply the trapped Wehrmacht forces by air.

Hitler did not understand at all what he was promising Paulus.

The scope of any relief mission, especially one that would require repeated drops of supplies over Stalingrad, would be enormous. The number of forces trapped in the city on the Volga was immense and varied. According to historian Charles Winchester:

> The entire 6th Army was there, the bulk of the 4th Panzer Army; 20 divisions belonging to four army corps and a Panzer corps. There were 13 infantry divisions, three Panzer divisions, three motorized divisions, a Luftwaffe flak division, field artillery regiments including two Sturmgeschutz battalions, a dozen combat engineer battalions, a Croat regiment attached to a Jager division, construction units, medical services, elements of the Reich's labor service, the 20th Romanian infantry and 1st Cavalry Division as well as survivors of the Romanian forces who had escaped eastwards into the pocket.

The Soviets had done their work well. They had cut off a large number of German and Axis forces and bottled them up in an urban wasteland from which escape, not to mention sheer survival, would be nearly impossible. One simple fact added one other huge obstacle to the equation: Paulus's forces in Stalingrad had only one week's worth of food and fuel left.

Even before the Soviet encirclement was complete, on November 22, Paulus sent a message to the German forces on the Don front: "Fuel will soon be exhausted. Tanks and heavy weapons then immovable. Ammunition situation strained. Food Provisions sufficient for six days. Army intends to hold remaining area from Stalingrad to Don." Confrontation broke out between Paulus and his corps commanders over what course of action should be taken. The commander of the 14th Panzer corps, the 4th corps, and the 11th corps believed that the best plan was to "obey Hitler and dig in." Paulus was desperate to try to break through the Soviet encirclement quickly. Only the promise of Luftwaffe support and an air supply line kept the Germans from accepting their fates as sealed.

That Luftwaffe support and the promised "air bridge" to Stalingrad never fully materialized, however. Hermann Göring, the head of the Luftwaffe, was called to meet with Hitler after the dictator had already promised air support to Paulus and his men. Not wanting to disappoint his leader and clearly understanding that Hitler was intent on keeping German forces in Stalingrad, he wanted to promise as much as he could. Even so, Göring knew that an airlift of adequate supplies to Paulus would be nearly impossible.

By Göring's estimates, the trapped 6th army would need "three hundred tons of fuel, 30 tons of munitions, and 150 tons of food" daily. To ship this incredible amount of supplies would require at least 800 Junkers JU-52 transport planes. The Luftwaffe did not even have that many planes in service. There were, in fact, only 750, and 100 of those were already being used to supply German forces in North Africa. Despite these facts, Hitler would not listen. "He told me that if we gathered all available transport planes, including Lufthansa civil planes, plus sufficient bombers, we could keep Stalingrad supplied," said Göring. Hitler could not be dissuaded: "I want everything, everything, do you hear, committed. If you use enough planes, we can easily keep Stalingrad supplied until the spring." Göring had no choice but to accept the German leader's orders.

The intervening months brought little relief to

Paulus. The airlift proved to be a failure. Even though many hundreds of planes were used for the resupply mission—Nazi leaders even offered their own private airplanes for the effort—the Russian antiaircraft guns shot them down regularly, causing the deaths of at least 1,000 airmen and the destruction of more than 600 aircraft. The harsh Soviet winter also grounded many relief planes. The result of these difficulties was that a woefully small amount of supplies was delivered to Paulus and his men. At the beginning of their entrapment, the 6 army had requested 500 tons (508 metric tons) of supplies daily. The amount was "a gross underestimation as Paulus . . . knew very well when he made it." Early Luftwaffe deliveries amounted to no more than 60 tons (61 metric tons) daily, and were later increased to 100 tons (102 metric tons). In reality, "the barest minimum quantity of supplies required by Paulus' troops was about 1,500 tons per day." This meant that the air bridge was short and inadequate, and was fighting a losing battle against time.

During the final week of November, Paulus dug his men into "a pocket measuring some 37 miles between Stalingrad and its western perimeter and 25 miles from north to south." In addition to the promise of air support and supplies, Hitler also informed Paulus that "Manstein will get you out." Field Marshal Erich von Manstein, commander of forces outside Leningrad, was, in late November, ordered to take command of army Group "Don," a new force that included the trapped 6th army and the Romanian 3rd army. Manstein was to "arrest the enemy's attacks and to regain the ground lost. . . ." After taking command of Group Don on November 26, two weeks passed before Manstein's forces were prepared to make an offensive move against the Soviets. In the meantime, the 23rd Panzer division had been rushed north from the Caucasus, and the 6th Panzer division had been delivered from France aboard 78 trains by November 27.

Despite these additions, Manstein's army was still too small. By December 10, when the German commander's forces began to move forward in an effort to launch an offensive toward Stalingrad, they did so with fewer than 500 armored vehicles. Field command was given to General Hermann Hoth, who had commanded the 1st Panzers in early months of the siege of Stalingrad.

Though some progress was made, including a forward movement of 50 miles (81 kilometers) of ground, the Soviets responded finally, on December 16, with "Operation Saturn," designed to place create a pincer movement of the southwest front and the Voronezh front and to destroy the Romanian 3rd army and the Italian 8th army. Zhukov was responsible for the coordination of the attack. Again, the Russians were able to move against their enemy with superior equipment and significant manpower. Russian tanks could even cross the Don River, since it was frozen solid enough to hold the heavy armored vehicles. Within 48 hours of the operation's launch on December 16, the Red army had broken through another center of German field resistance. By December 23, Manstein pulled his forces back across the Don River, having failed completely to rout the Russians.

In the field, Manstein, like Paulus, who was still locked up in Stalingrad, was short on supplies, including food and fuel. His men were eating rice and horse meat. By the last day of December, Red army forces had driven Hoth and his Panzers back to where they had started on the Don River, and had brought about the collapse of the German defensive front along the same river. These events left the German army in the Caucasus isolated.

As the Soviets extended their stranglehold on the Germans in Stalingrad, there was little immediate panic among the forces of the Wehrmacht in and around the city. Despite the desperate circumstances the German 6th army faced during a cold December, the army's "discipline and organization . . . remained excellent." Military traffic moved reasonably well, the limited supplies that were on hand were doled out with efficiency, and hospitals managed to run, despite the fact that casualties were entering at a rate of 1,500 per day. Food was becoming a major problem, though. Soldiers of the 6th army began to die of starvation on December 9, when two "simply fell down and died." Other such deaths followed. At the start of January, the daily ration for Paulus and his men was next to nothing: 2.5 ounces (71 grams) of bread, 7 ounces (198 grams) of horse meat, including the bones, less than half an ounce (14 grams) of fat and sugar each. The cold made the terrible circumstances even more unbearable. As had happened the previous year, when German troops laid siege to Moscow and Leningrad even though they had no winter uniforms, the Wehrmacht forces in Stalingrad also faced the bitter cold without warm clothing.

Paulus and his men were being abandoned. They were exhausted beyond reason. Many of them were unable to stand and march, must less fight. Diseases such as dysentery and typhoid fever struck whole units and spread like wildfire. The troops faced temperatures between -20° F and -30° F (-29° C and -34° C). Wounded soldiers lying on operating tables sometimes froze to death before they could be seen by a doctor. Paulus conveyed his emotions to a major on his staff: "Could you ever imagine soldiers falling on a dead horse, cutting off its head, and devouring its brains raw? How can we go on fighting when the men haven't even got winter clothing?"

At the beginning of January, the situation grew worse for the Germans trapped in Stalingrad. Russian planes continually strafed infantry units from the air. They bombed any target they considered strategic, even individual trucks. Russian infantry and tank units made further advances, driving their helpless enemy deeper into Stalingrad. Everywhere, everything was breaking down for the Germans:

> German soldiers had begun to desert in large numbers; many officers in the field had lost the will to lead. Blankets over their heads, the men slept at sentry posts; without tanks behind them as support, terrified Germans now ran in the face of the enemy assaults. . . . [T]he general feeling in the pocket had become one of simple self-preservation.

Some desperate officers and enlisted men even committed suicide.

On January 9, the Soviets offered to accept a surrender from Paulus, but he rejected the proposal outright. Still, the Germans' plight continued to worsen. As discipline among the troops deteriorated, Paulus responded, ordering "364 of his men shot for cowardice in just one week."

On January 10, the Soviets launched a massive artillery assault on the 6th army. Seven thousand guns and mortars were unleashed in an attempt to bring about the surrender of the last of Hitler's forces in and west of Stalingrad. After an hour of constant barrage, Red army ground forces were sent forward to attack. During the next week, the Soviets captured two-thirds of the section of Stalingrad where the 6th army had been holed up since November.

By January 22, Paulus sent a message to Hitler, requesting that he be allowed to surrender:

> After having repelled . . . massive enemy attacks . . . all ammunition has been exhausted. Russians advancing on both sides of Voroponvo on a 6-kilometer front. . . . No longer any chance of stemming the flood. Neighboring fronts, also without any ammunition, contracting. Sharing ammunition with other fronts no longer feasible either. Food running out. More than 12,000 wounded in the pocket untended. What orders should I issue to troops who have no more ammunition and are under continuous attack from masses of artillery, tanks, and infantry? Immediate reply essential as signs of collapse already evident in places.

Although the Luftwaffe had managed to evacuate nearly 35,000 wounded men out of the Stalingrad region during the siege, tens of thousands more were left behind. As the final days of the siege arrived, Paulus made another desperate, yet seemingly practical decision: The wounded would receive no more food rations.

Having read Paulus's desperate message, Hitler remained unmoved. He refused to allow his field commander to surrender. Russian actions on January 26 resulted in the division of the 6th army and the capture of the rest of its pocket. On the southern end of the city, the commander of the German 71st division was killed in action. The general of the 113th killed himself. Other commanders surrendered without permission from

By January 1943, realizing that the fight was lost, many German soldiers surrendered to the Soviets, regardless of the commands of their superiors.

Paulus or Hitler. By January 30, from his headquarters in the basement of what had formerly been Stalingrad's grandest department store, Univermag, Paulus himself made his ultimate decision without approval from Hitler: He surrendered his 6th army. In the city of Moscow, far to the north, the bells of the Kremlin rang out the message of the Soviet victory at Stalingrad.

Back at his headquarters, now in Berlin, Adolf Hitler learned of Paulus's surrender and went into a rage, shouting that "Paulus and his staff had dishonored

Despite Adolf Hitler's orders to the contrary, Field Marshal Paulus decided to surrender his troops to the Soviets at the end of January 1943. Paulus is seen here on his way to make his formal surrender.

themselves by preferring surrender to suicide." Within a week, however, Hitler, who had drawn a line in the sand and ordered his men to hold an unholdable city, became reflective, even realistic, and took responsibility for his errors in military judgment. General Manstein, who was called to Hitler's headquarters on February 6, recorded Hitler's words: "As for Stalingrad, I alone bear the responsibility."

Epilogue

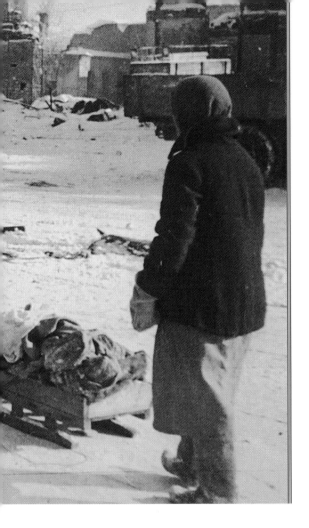

By the end of the siege, Stalingrad had been reduced to a pile of rubble and its people had fled the city as refugees.

In the aftermath of the German surrender by early February 1943, both sides were forced to take count of their losses. Nearly 150,000 German and Romanian soldiers had died during the nearly three months they were trapped in Stalingrad. The Soviets had nearly 50,000 dead, but on the positive side, the Red army had accepted the surrender of 91,000 Axis forces, including 24 generals and 2,500 other officers. Six thousand German artillery pieces had been captured, nearly all without any reserve ammunition. Sixty thousand motorized vehicles of war fell in the hands of the victorious Soviet army.

As for the city itself, it hardly existed in any way other than in name. From September 1942 through January 1943, during

115

the battle for Stalingrad, "99 percent of the city had been reduced to rubble." The list of urban structures destroyed was staggering, including 41,000 homes, 300 factories, and 113 hospitals and schools. When the siege of Stalingrad began, the city on the Volga had been home to nearly half a million residents. By February 1943, only 1,515 of the original residents were left. All the others had either fled east to safety in Siberia or had been killed in the fight for the city.

As for the German 6th army, which had pushed the British and French to the coast at Dunkirk in the summer of 1940—it had been destroyed. Its remaining members were shipped off to desolate prison camps across the Soviet Union, including the frozen reaches of the Arctic. They were force-marched, indiscriminately shot, or starved. Many froze to death. They died as diseases swept through their camps. In some prison camps, the nearly dead survivors of the grand 6th army that had marched across the entire span of Europe practiced cannibalism as their comrades died—and sometimes even before.

The heroes of the valiant stand against German aggression, General Chuikov and his 62nd army left the city to rest and recover east of the Volga. Their reprieve lasted only a few weeks, however. In a short time, the 62nd was back on active duty, renamed the 8th guards. The unit did not stop fighting for the next two years, until it had successfully besieged another city, this one in Germany— Berlin. During the war, Chuikov was decorated lavishly by the Soviet Union, and after the war, he was appointed commander of all Soviet land forces.

That spring of 1943, as Chuikov and his men left the city they had defended so courageously, the weary Red army leader wondered if he would ever see Stalingrad again. In later years, he recalled his thoughts: "Goodbye, Volga. Goodbye the tortured and devastated city. Will we ever see you again and what will you be like? Goodbye, our friends, lie in peace in the land soaked with the blood of our people."

1914–1918	The years spanning World War I. During this international conflict, Czarist Russia and the Empire of Germany were at war with one another. 1917—Russian Revolution removes the last of the Romanov czars, Nicholas II, from his throne, and establishes a pro-communist government.
1918	German occupy extensive Russian territory. The Germans forced the Russians to accept defeat under the Treaty of Brest-Litovsk.
1918–1921	Russian civil war which pitted Bolshevik (or Red) forces of Lenin against the White (or anti-Bolshevik) Army. By 1921, Bolsheviks had defeated the Whites and spread communism to neighbors, including the Ukraine, White Russia, the Trans-Caucasia, and Siberia.
1919	Communist leader, V.I. Lenin establishes the Union of Soviet Socialist Republics. That same year, the Allied victors of World War I force the Germans to accept responsibility for the war, as well as the Treaty of Versailles.

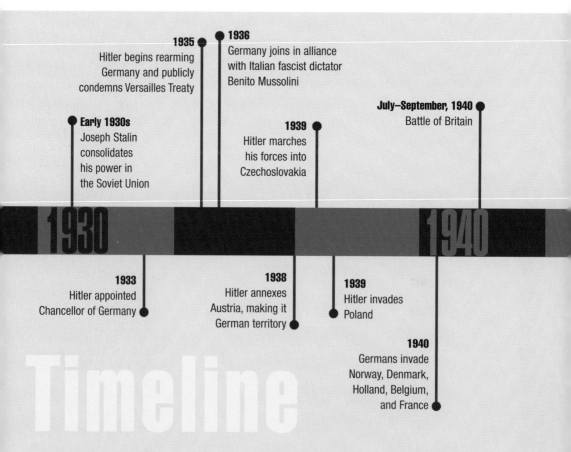

1935 Hitler begins rearming Germany and publicly condemns Versailles Treaty

1936 Germany joins in alliance with Italian fascist dictator Benito Mussolini

July–September, 1940 Battle of Britain

Early 1930s Joseph Stalin consolidates his power in the Soviet Union

1939 Hitler marches his forces into Czechoslovakia

1930

1940

1933 Hitler appointed Chancellor of Germany

1938 Hitler annexes Austria, making it German territory

1939 Hitler invades Poland

1940 Germans invade Norway, Denmark, Holland, Belgium, and France

Timeline

1920	Joseph Stalin fights off several White Army assaults against Volga city of Tsaritsyn, which will later be renamed "Stalingrad."
Early 1920s	Bavarian Adolf Hitler forms a party of political agitators called the National Socialist German Workers Party, known to many as the Nazis.
1923	Hitler's Nazi Party attempts a take over of the government of Bavaria, in Austria, but the efforts fails. Hitler is jailed for a year.
1924	The German Weimar government cracks down on subversive political groups, such as the National Socialists.
1929	The Nazi Party is the most important, well-known minority political group in Germany.
1932	Hitler's National Socialists win a majority of seats in the German legislature.
Early 1930s	Joseph Stalin consolidates his power in the Soviet Union.
1933	Hitler is appointed as Chancellor of Germany. Before the year is over, he consolidates his power, and withdraws Germany from the League of Nations.

June, 1941
Stalin annexes Baltic states of Lithuania, Latvia, and Estonia

September 13, 1942
Germans launch a series of massive attacks on Stalingrad

October 14, 1942
Another German offensive is launched on Stalingrad; German forces attack Tractor Factory and Barrikady Gun Factory

June 22, 1941
Germany unleashes blitzkrieg against Soviet Union

September 12, 1942
Soviet General Yeremenko appoints new commander of Russian 62nd Army— Gen. Vassili Chuikov

Jaunuary 30, 1943
German 6th Army surrenders to Soviet forces, and siege of Stalingrad ends

1941   **1943**

Fall, 1941
Germans lay siege to Leningrad and Moscow, but fail to bring down either city

April 5, 1942
Hitler issues Fuhrer Directive No. 41, ordering offensive against Stalingrad

August 24, 1942
German attacks on Stalingrad commence with air and troop movements

November 23, 1942
Russians successfully encircle 300,000 Germans trapped in Stalingrad

July 21, 1942
Stalingrad city officials receive order from Stalin for every man, woman, and child to help fortify the city

November 19, 1942
Soviets launch counter-offensive "Operation Uranus" and within days, Germans lose extensive ground

1935	Hitler calls for the rearming of Germany, while he publicly condemns the Versailles Treaty.
1936	The German leader joins in an alliance with another fascist leader, Benito Mussolini, military dictator of Italy. They form the Rome-Berlin Axis.
1938	Hitler takes command of all German military forces and immediately orders them to march against nations to the east. Before year's end, Hitler is granted control of the Sudetenland, at the expense of Czechoslovakia.

1938

March 13	Hitler annexes Austria, making it German territory. Western Europe powers, including Great Britain and France, manage only a weak protest.

1939

March	Hitler marches his forces into the whole of Czechoslovakia.
September 1	Germany invades Poland.
September 3	Great Britain and France declare war on Germany.

1940

Spring–Summer	Germans invade Norway, Denmark, Holland, Belgium, and France.
Mid-July–September	Battle of Britain is fought, as Germany attempts to invade the British Isles by air and sea. Hitler's Operation Sea Lion is eventually postponed indefinitely.
November–March, 1941	Russo-Finnish War.

1941

Spring	Hitler plans to attack the Soviet Union despite a non-aggression agreement between the two countries.
April	Germany invades Yugoslavia. With the fall of Yugoslavia, Greece falls into German hands within days.
June	Soviet leader, Stalin, annexes the defenseless Baltic states of Lithuania, Latvia, and Estonia, followed by the seizure of Bessarabia.
June 22	Germans unleash blitzkrieg against the unsuspecting Soviet Union, catching Stalin off-guard.
September	German Army Group North has reached the outskirts of the Soviet city of Leningrad.
October 20	Germans have advanced to just 40 miles outside of the Soviet city of Moscow.

Fall	German armies lay siege to Moscow and Leningrad. The cities face absolute desperation as food supplies dwindle, causing massive starvation, yet the Russians manage to hold out in both cities, leaving the Germans inside the Soviet Union as winter arrives.
November	Germans are trapped inside the Soviet Union by a harsh Russian winter. Germany has now experienced 750,000 casualties on its Soviet campaign, including 200,000 killed.
December 5	Soviet General Zhukov orders the movement of multiple Russian counter-attacks against the German forces inside the Soviet Union. After only three weeks of fighting, the Soviets have regained nearly all the territory the Germans had captured.

1942

January	By this month, the German offensive has proven expensive, including the loss of three out of every four tanks the Germans sent into the Soviet Union, as well as 2,000 Luftwaffe planes destroyed.
Spring	Both the Russians and the Germans rebuild their forces in preparation for a return to hostilities by early summer.
April 5	Hitler issues Fuhrer Directive No. 41, which calls for multiple, offensive field movements by the German military in the Crimean, the Caucasus, and against the city of Stalingrad.
May 12	The Russians attempt to rout the German 6th and 17th Armies from their positions at key crossing junctures along the Dnieper River in the Ukraine.
July 3	The Germans occupy the Crimean city of Sevastopol.
June 28	The German 4th Panzer hits a Russian rail junction near the town of Voronezh, on the Volga River. Germans advancing on Stalingrad are within 200 miles of the city.
July 21	City officials in Stalingrad receive orders from Stalin to have every man, woman, and child working on establishing a fortification complex around Stalingrad.
July 30	Fourth Panzers and German 6th Army are reunited outside Stalingrad.
August 5	The 4th Panzer Army captures an important rail center just 73 miles southwest of Stalingrad. The German 6th Army had advanced to Kalatsch, on the Don River, just 30 miles due west of Stalingrad.

August 12–13   Stalin meets with British Prime Minister Winston Churchill in Moscow to discuss the establishment of a second major front in France. Churchill makes it clear to Stalin the Allies will not establish such a front until 1943.

August 23   Several German tank corps, including the 16th and 14th Panzers complete a spectacular run north of the city and reach the town of Rynok, with Stalingrad just a few miles to the south. Sixth Army commander, Paulus, establishes a forty-mile-long front from the Don River to the Volga.

August 24   German attacks on the city of Stalingrad commence, from the air and through troop movements. Before day's end, the 16th Panzer Division, is positioned on the edge of the city.

August 27   Stalin, from his headquarters in Moscow, dispatches Marshal Georgi Zhukov, veteran of the Leningrad siege, to Stalingrad as the new commander of Red Army forces in the city.

August 29   Zhukov arrives in Stalingrad.

August 31   Within one week, the German Luftwaffe had managed to destroy 100 downtown city blocks of Stalingrad.

September 12   Soviet General Yeremenko appoints new commander of the Russian 62nd Army—General Vassili Chuikov. When Chuikov takes command, the 62nd numbers just 50,000 men.

September– October   Germans and Russians engage in bitter street fighting for control of the beleaguered city of Stalingrad.

September 13   Germans launch a series of massive attacks on the city of Stalingrad, in a desperate attempt to take control and rout out the last of Russian forces. For the immediate days, the offensive is challenged by stiff Soviet resistance.

September 28   Stalin approves "Operation Uranus" which includes plans for a massive counter-offensive to be launched by the Red Army against German forces inside the Soviet Union.

October 14   Another German offensive is launched on a massive scale. German 6th Army forces are sent against the Dzerhezinsky Tractor Factory and the Barrikady Gun Factory complex. During the following four days, the two armies fought for control of the city.

October 18   Some German units are now within 300 yards of the Volga River. Germans are in the vicinity of the Red October Factory.

November 11 The German 6th Army launches attacks against the Red October Factory, blitzing the grounds with nine concentrated divisions. But elements of the 6th are completely worn out, battle weary, and drastically reduced in numbers.

November 19 Soviets launch massive counter-offensive, "Operation Uranus." Within days, the Germans begin to lose ground on several combined fronts. German units begin to fall into Soviet hands.

November 22 Just three days after the Russian counter-offensive is launched, some Red Army units have advanced forward as many as 60 miles. The Russians capture the main bridge spanning the Don River.

November 23 The Russians have successfully encircled more than 300,000 German forces, including the entire 6th Army, within the confines of Stalingrad itself. Hitler refuses to allow General Paulus to order a breakout of German troops in an attempt to escape from Stalingrad.

December 9 First German soldiers fall to starvation inside Stalingrad.

December 10 German rescue offensive is launched to help free Paulus and his forces in Stalingrad.

December 16 Soviets launch "Operation Saturn," designed to create a pincer movement of the South-West Front and the Voronezh Front and utterly destroy the Romanian 3rd Army and the Italian 8th Army situated west of Stalingrad. The offensive is a success.

December 23 German rescue offensive is called off as Wehrmacht forces meet with stiff resistance and fail to rout the Russians.

December 31 All German fronts have failed in the vicinity of Stalingrad.

1943

January 9 Soviets offer to accept surrender from Field Marshal (newly promoted) Paulus, who rejects offer outright.

January 10 Soviets launch a massive artillery assault on the 6th Army and their positions inside Stalingrad.

January 22 Field Marshal Paulus sends message to Hitler requesting he be allowed to surrender to the Russians. Hitler refuses.

January 26 Russian troop actions result in the division of the 6th Army and its pocket inside Stalingrad.

January 30 From his headquarters in the bombed-out Univermag Department Store, Field Marshal Paulus surrenders his 6th Army.

CHAPTER 1: A STAGE SET FOR WAR

Page 7: "grenades exploded . . ." William Craig. *Enemy at the Gates: The Battle for Stalingrad*. New York: E. P. Dutton & Co., Inc., 1973, p. 97.

Page 11: "German divisions had dealt . . ." Gregory Freeze. *Russia, A History*. New York: Oxford University Press, p. 233.

Page 12: "one-third of Russia's . . ." John Keegan. *The Second World War*. New York: Viking, 1989, p. 26.

Page 15: "I thought of nothing . . ." Ibid., p. 31.

Page 20–21: "The Nazi-Soviet pact . . ." Stephen Ambrose. *American Heritage New History of World War II*. New York: Viking, 1997, p. 39.

Page 24: "The Finns had fortified . . ." Charles Winchester. *Ostfront: Hitler's War on Russia, 1941–45*. Oxford, UK: Osprey Publishing, 2000, p. 30.

Page 26: "the German High Command's . . ." Ibid., p. 31.

Page 27: "ordered the disarming . . ." Ibid.

CHAPTER 2: WAR ENGULFS A CONTINENT

Page 30: "Had I known they . . ." Keegan, p. 215.

Page 32: "was to advance . . ." Charles Winchester. *Ostfront: Hitler's War on Russia, 1941–45*. Oxford, UK: Osprey Publishing, 2000, p. 33.

Page 32: "The German armies had not . . ." Ibid.

Page 33–34: "At approximately 3:00 a.m. . . ." Nicholas Bethell. *Russia Besieged*. Alexandria, VA: TIME-Life Books, 1977, p. 30.

Page 35: "swallowing hair oil . . ." Stephen Ambrose. *American Heritage New History of World War II*. New York: Viking, 1997, p. 239.

Page 38: "double envelopment . . ." Keegan, p. 202.

Page 39: "The myth of invincibility . . ." Ambrose, p. 238.

Page 41: "Behind the Russian lines . . ." Winchester, p. 55.

Page 42: " . . . Hitler's plans for . . . " Ambrose, p. 243.

CHAPTER 3: HITLER PLOTS HIS STRATEGY

Page 45: "twenty infantry and seven . . ." James L. Collins. *The Marshall Cavendish Illustrated Encyclopedia of World War II*, vol. 7. New York: Marshall Cavendish, 1972, p. 912.

Page 46: "the biggest gun ever . . ." Charles Winchester. *Ostfront: Hitler's War on Russia, 1941–45*. Oxford, UK: Osprey Publishing, 2000, p. 58.

Page 47: "That he would continue . . ." Ibid.

Page 49: "could not believe . . ." William Craig. *Enemy at the Gates: The Battle for Stalingrad*. New York: E. P. Dutton & Co., Inc., 1973, p. 20.

Page 51: "operation's ultimate goal . . ." Craig, p. 25.

Page 51–52: "so many precious days . . ." Ibid., p. 21.

Page 52: "close on two enemy . . ." Ibid.

Page 53–54: "We have lost 70 million . . ." Collins, vol. 7, p. 921.

Page 55: "that still in 1942 . . ." Walter Kerr. *The Secret of Stalingrad*. Garden City, NY: Doubleday & Company, Inc., 1978, p. 89.

CHAPTER 4: THE CITY ON THE VOLGA

Page 58: "Despite the boom, the city . . ." William Craig. *Enemy at the Gates: The Battle for Stalingrad*. New York: E. P. Dutton & Co., Inc., 1973, p. 29.

Page 59: "looked like a giant caterpillar . . ." Ibid., p. 30.

Page 59: "a maze of foundries . . ." Ibid., p. 36.

Page 61: "a philharmonic orchestra . . ." Ibid., p. 35.

Page 61: "underwear, socks, trousers . . ." Ibid.

Page 62: "To the west, there was . . ." Ibid., p. 36.

Page 62: "Thanks to the brave advance . . ." Ibid., p. 41.

Page 63: "In contrast to Waterloo . . ." Walter Kerr. *The Secret of Stalingrad*. Garden City, NY: Doubleday & Company, Inc., 1978, p. 85.

Page 65: "he inched his way forward . . ." Ibid., p. 72.

Page 65: "stopped Hoth and drove him . . ." Ibid., p. 93.

Page 65: "The closer the enemy got . . ." Ibid.

Page 66: "The Russians naturally wanted . . ." Thomas Heyck. The Peoples of the British Isles. p. 247.

Page 67: "the Soviet command built their plan . . ." Kerr, p. 105.

Page 67: "In short, two days of talks . . ." Ibid., p. 107.

Page 68: "followed tramcars down . . ." Craig, p. 52.

Page 68: "forty-mile-long corridor . . ." Ibid., p. 63.

CHAPTER 5: FIGHTING IN THE STREETS

Page 71: "compact columns of trucks . . ." William Craig. *Enemy at the Gates: The Battle for Stalingrad*. New York: E. P. Dutton & Co., Inc., 1973, p. 54.

Page 71: "Whoever can bear arms . . ." Ibid., p. 56.

Page 72: "Concussions blew down most . . ." Ibid., p. 58.

Page 73: "the situation was very bad . . ." Ibid., p. 62.

Page 73: "Evacuation and mining . . ." Ibid.

Page 76–77: "Living in foxholes. . ." Craig, p. 123.

Page 77: "withering fire from . . ." Ibid., p. 64.

Page 78: "faced the chilling prospect . . ." Ibid., p. 66.

Page 78: "With no place to hide . . ." Ibid., p. 71.

Page 79: "Many deserters, some even . . ." Ibid., p. 72.

Page 81: "trucks, tanks, and hundreds . . ." Ibid., p. 76.

Page 82:   "went into a tirade . . ." Ibid., p. 80.

Page 82:   "Germans had the brains . . ." Walter Kerr.
            The Secret of Stalingrad. Garden City, NY:
            Doubleday & Company, Inc., 1978, p. 148.

Page 83:   "frequently mistaken for . . ." Craig, p. 84.

Page 83:   "An armored brigade . . ." Ibid.

Page 84:   "did not depend on strength . . ." James L.
            Collins. *The Marshall Cavendish Illustrated
            Encyclopedia of World War II*, vol. 8. New
            York: Marshall Cavendish, 1972, p. 983.

Page 84:   "There were times when . . ." Kerr, p. 182.

Page 84:   "0730 [7:30 A.M.] the enemy . . ." Collins,
            vol. 8, p. 983.

Page 89:   "The Street is no longer measured . . ."
            Stephen Ambrose. *American Heritage New
            History of World War II*. New York:
            Viking, 1997, p. 247.

CHAPTER 6: TURNING THE TIDE OF BATTLE

Page 91:   "the incompetent meddling of . . ."
            Mikhail Heller and Aleksandr M.
            Nekrich. *Utopia Power: The History of
            the Soviet Union From 1917 to the Present*.
            New York: Summit Books, 1986.

Page 92:   "every night hundreds of ferries . . ."
            James L. Collins. *The Marshall Cavendish
            Illustrated Encyclopedia of World War II*,
            vol. 8. New York: Marshall Cavendish,
            1972, p. 985.

Page 93:   "It was like a boxer . . ." Stephen Ambrose.
            *American Heritage New History of World
            War II*. New York: Viking, 1997, p. 247.

Page 93:   "for a full-scale counter-offensive . . ."
            Charles Winchester. *Ostfront: Hitler's War
            on Russia, 1941–45*. Oxford, UK: Osprey
            Publishing, 2000, p. 66.

Page 94:   "[The] battle for the city . . ." Ibid., p. 67.

Page 95:   "not just cut off the Germans . . ." Ibid.

Page 95:   "The plan of the Soviet command . . ."
            Heller and Nekrich, p. 400.

Page 95:   "major formations including . . ." Collins,
            vol. 8, p. 989.

Page 96:   "On 14 October the Germans . . ." John
            Keegan. *The Second World War*. New
            York: Viking, 1989, p. 231.

Page 96:   "For every house, workshop, . . ." Ibid.,
            p. 230.

Page 96:   "The fighting raged day . . ." Winchester,
            p. 69.

Page 98:   "We had no idea of the . . ." Collins, vol. 8,
            p. 991.

Page 98:   "deduced that the enemy . . ." Ibid., p. 992.

Page 98:   "he could do no more . . ." Ibid.

Page 98:   "the thunderous roar . . ." Winchester, p. 70.

Page 101:   "found tables laden . . ." Collins, vol. 8,
            pp. 999–1000.

Page 101:   "I won't go back from . . ." Skipper, G.C.
            World at War: Battle of Stalingrad. Chicago:
            Children's Press, 21.

CHAPTER 7: NO WAY OUT

Page 103:   "temporary encirclement" Bullock, *Alan.
            Hitler and Stalin, Parallel Lives*. New York:
            Alfred A Knopf, 787.

Page 104:   "The entire 6th Army was where . . ."
            Winchester, 70.

Page 104:   "Fuel will soon be exhausted. . ." Ibid.

Page 105:   "obey Hitler and dig in. . ." Ibid.

Page 105:   "three hundred tons of fuel. . ." Mosley,
            Leonard. *The Reich Marshall: A Biography
            of Hermann Goering*. Garden City, NY:
            Doubleday & Company, Inc., 323.

Page 105:   "He told me that if we. . ." Ibid.

Page 105:   "I want everything. . ." Ibid.

Page 106:   "a gross underestimation. . ." Winchester,
            73

Page 106:   "the barest minimum quantity. . ." Ibid.

Page 106:   "a pocket measuring. . ." Collins, Vol. 8,
            1005.

Page 106:   "Manstein will get you out. . ." Winchester,
            71.

Page 106:   "arrest the enemy's attacks. . ." Collins,
            Vol 8, 1005-06.

Page 108:   "discipline and organization. . ." Craig, 233.

Page 108:   "simply fell down and died. . ." Ibid.

Page 109:   "Could you ever imagine. . ." Collins,
            Vol. 8, 1008.

Page 109:   "German soldiers had begun. . ." Craig,
            343.

Page 109:   364 of his men shot. . ." Winchester, 78.

Page 110:   "After having repelled. . ." Collins, Vol. 9,
            1221.

Page 111:   "Paulus and his staff. . ." Ibid., 1223.

EPILOGUE

Page 116:   "99 percent of the city had. . ." Craig, 392.

Page 117:   "Goodbye, Volga. Goodbye. . ." Keegan,
            236.

Ambrose, Stephen E. *American Heritage New History of World War II*. New York: Viking, 1997.

Beevor, Antony. *Stalingrad: The Fateful Siege, 1942–1943*. New York: Penguin Putnam Inc., 1999.

Bethell, Nicholas. *Russia Besieged*. Alexandria, VA: TIME-Life Books, 1977.

Bialer, Seweryn. *Stalin and His Generals: Soviet Military Memoirs of World War II*. New York: Pegasus, 1969.

Bullock, Alan. *Hitler and Stalin, Parallel Lives*. New York: Alfred A. Knopf, 1992.

Carell, Paul. *Stalingrad: The Defeat of the German 6 Army*. Atglen, PA: Schiffer Publishing, Ltd., 1993.

Collins, James L., ed. *The Marshall Cavendish Illustrated Encyclopedia of World War II. Volumes 6-9*. New York: Marshall Cavendish, 1972.

Craig, William. *Enemy at the Gates: The Battle for Stalingrad*. New York: E. P. Dutton & Co., Inc., 1973.

Cross, Robin. *Warfare, A Chronological History*. Secaucus, NJ: Wellfleet Press, 1991.

Dupuy, R. Ernest. *World War II, A Compact History*. New York: Hawthorn Books, Inc., 1969.

Erickson, John. *The Road to Stalingrad: Stalin's War With Germany, Volume I*. New Haven, CT: Yale University Press, 1999.

Heller, Mikhail, and Aleksandr M. Nekrich. *Utopia Power: The History of the Soviet Union From 1917 to the Present*. New York: Summit Books, 1986.

Higgins, Trumbull. *Hitler and Russia: The Third Reich in a Two-Front War, 1937–1943*. New York: Macmillan Company, 1966.

Keegan, John. *The Second World War*. New York: Viking, 1989.

Kerr, Walter. *The Secret of Stalingrad*. Garden City, NY: Doubleday & Company, Inc., 1978.

Mosley, Leonard. *The Reich Marshall: A Biography of Hermann Goering*. Garden City, NY: Doubleday & Company, Inc., 1974.

Natkiel, Richard. *Atlas of World War II*. New York: The Military Press, 1985.

Seaton, Albert. *Stalin as Military Commander*. New York: Praeger Publishers, 1975.

Speer, Albert. *Inside the Third Reich*. New York: Macmillan Company, 1970.

Toland, John. *Adolf Hitler*. Garden City, NY: Doubleday & Company, Inc., 1976.

Ulam, Adam B. *Stalin: The Man and His Era*. New York: Viking Press, 1973.

Walsh, Stephen. *Stalingrad: The Infernal Cauldron*. New York: St. Martin's Press, Inc., 2001.

Winchester, Charles. *Ostfront: Hitler's War on Russia, 1941–45*. Oxford, UK: Osprey Publishing, 2000.

TIM McNEESE is an Associate Professor of History at York College in Nebraska. He is the author of more than fifty books and educational materials on everything from Egyptian pyramids to American Indians. Professor McNeese graduated from York College with his Associate of Arts degree, as well as Harding University where he received his Bachelor of Arts degree in history and political science. He received his Master of Arts degree in history from Southwest Missouri State University. His audiences range from elementary students to adults. He is currently in his 27th year of teaching. Professor McNeese's writing career has earned him a citation in the "Something About the Author" reference work. He is married to Beverly McNeese who teaches English at York College.